First French
Dictionary

REVISED EDITION
Editors Olivia Stanford, Anwesha Dutta, Shambhavi Thatte, Shalini Agrawal
Senior art editor Ann Cannings
Art editors Jaileen Kaur, Kartik Gera
Senior editor Marie Greenwood
Editorial assistant Amina Youssef
US Senior editor Shannon Beatty
US Editor Elizabeth Searcy
DTP designers Bimlesh Tiwary, Jaypal Singh Chauhan, Vikram Singh
Jacket co-ordinator Francesca Young
Jacket designer Suzena Sengupta
Managing editors Laura Gilbert, Alka Thakur Hazarika
Managing art editors Diane Peyton Jones, Romi Chakraborty
CTS manager Balwant Singh
Senior producer, pre-production Nadine King
Producer Isabell Schart
Art director Martin Wilson
Publishing director Sarah Larter

Translator Vasanti Piette

ORIGINAL EDITION
Project editor Anna Harrison
Editor Elise See Tai
Project art editors Ann Cannings, Emy Manby
DTP Designer David McDonald
Production Harriet Maxwell
Translator Chantal Lamarque with Elise Bradbury
Managing editor Scarlett O'Hara

First American Edition, 2005
Published in the United States by DK Publishing
345 Hudson Street, New York, New York 10014

Copyright © 2005, © 2009,
© 2015, © 2018
Dorling Kindersley Limited
DK, a Division of Penguin Random House LLC
18 19 20 21 22 10 9 8 7 6 5 4 3 2 1
001-307944-Mar/2018

A catalog record for this book is available from the Library of Congress.
ISBN: 978-1-4654-7003-4

DK books are available at special discounts when purchased in bulk for sales promotions, premiums, fund-raising, or educational use. For details, contact: DK Publishing Special Markets, 345 Hudson Street, New York, New York 10014
SpecialSales@dk.com

Printed and bound in China

A WORLD OF IDEAS:
SEE ALL THERE IS TO KNOW

www.dk.com

Contents

There is a question at the bottom of each topic page...

How to use this dictionary

At the beginning of the book there are topic pages. These include lots of useful words on a particular subject, such as "Pets" and "In the park." Each word has a translation and instructions on how to pronounce it. The words on the topic pages can be found in the English A–Z and in the French A–Z. There are lots of other useful words here, too. The verbs section can be found after the A–Zs. At the back of the book there is a list of useful phrases to help you practice French with your friends. On page 113 you will find a pronunciation guide.

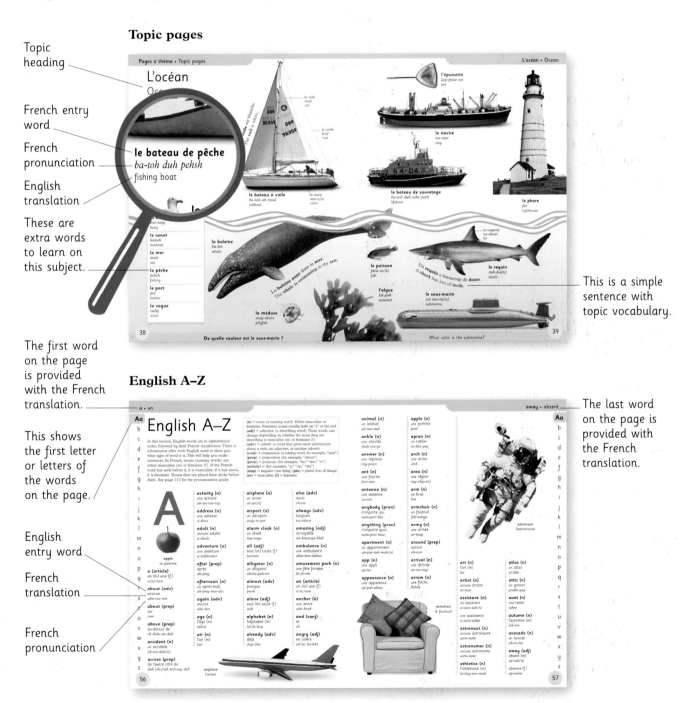

Topic heading

French entry word

French pronunciation

English translation

These are extra words to learn on this subject.

Topic pages

Pages à thème • Topic pages

L'océan
Ocean

le bateau de pêche
ba-toh duh pehsh
fishing boat

le bateau à voile
ba-toh ah vwal
sailboat

The first word on the page is provided with the French translation.

English A–Z

This shows the first letter or letters of the words on the page.

English entry word

French translation

French pronunciation

This is a simple sentence with topic vocabulary.

The last word on the page is provided with the French translation.

...check here for the translation.

Tout à mon sujet
All about me

Je suis grande.
I am tall.

Voici ma famille.
Here is my family.

le bébé
bay-bay
baby

le père
pair
father

la mère
mair
mother

l'enfant
lahn-fah(n)
child

la sœur
suhr
sister

le frère
frair
brother

Extra words to learn

les amis
a-mee
friends

le beau-père
boh pair
stepfather

la belle-mère
bel mair
stepmother

le demi-frère
duh-mi frair
stepbrother

la demi-sœur
duh-mi suhr
stepsister

le grand-père
grahn pair
grandfather

la grand-mère
grahn mair
grandmother

les grands-parents
grah(n) par-ah(n)
grandparents

la tante
tahnt
aunt

l'oncle
lonk-luh
uncle

De quelle couleur sont tes yeux ?

Extra words to learn

les cheveux
shuh-vuh
hair

le cou
koo
neck

le coude
kood
elbow

la dent
dah(n)
tooth

le dos
do
back

la famille
fa-mee-ye
family

le genou
zhuh-noo
knee

le sourcil
soor-seel
eyebrow

le visage
vee-zazh
face

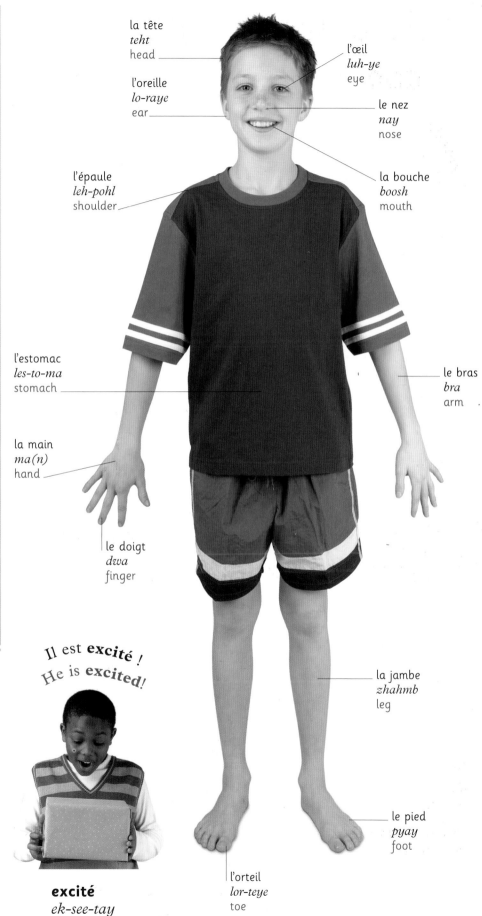

la tête
teht
head

l'œil
luh-ye
eye

l'oreille
lo-raye
ear

le nez
nay
nose

l'épaule
leh-pohl
shoulder

la bouche
boosh
mouth

l'estomac
les-to-ma
stomach

le bras
bra
arm

la main
ma(n)
hand

le doigt
dwa
finger

la jambe
zhahmb
leg

le pied
pyay
foot

l'orteil
lor-teye
toe

Je **pleure** quand je suis **triste**.
I **cry** when I am **sad**.

triste
treest
sad

Il est **excité** !
He is **excited**!

excité
ek-see-tay
excited

Les vêtements
Clothes

les chaussettes
shoh-set
socks

le bouton
boo-to(n)
button

la chemise
shuh-meez
shirt

le jean
jeen
jeans

**Extra words
to learn**

la ceinture
sehn-ture
belt

la chaussure
shoh-soor
shoe

les lunettes
lew-net
glasses

la pantoufle
pahn-too-fluh
slipper

le pull
pewl
sweater

le pyjama
pee-zha-ma
pajamas

la robe
rob
dress

les sous-vêtements
soo veht-mah(n)
underwear

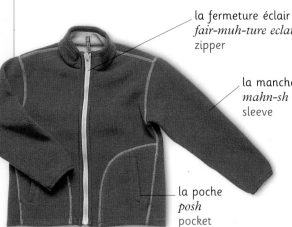

la fermeture éclair
fair-muh-ture eclair
zipper

la manche
mahn-sh
sleeve

la poche
posh
pocket

la polaire
po-lair
fleece

Mon **manteau** me tient **chaud**.
My **coat** keeps me **warm**.

l'écharpe
lay-sharp
scarf

le gant
gah(n)
glove

le manteau
mahn-toh
coat

les baskets
bas-ket
sneakers

Aimes-tu porter des baskets ?

le tee-shirt
tee shirt
T-shirt

le pantalon
pahn-ta-lo(n)
pants

le short
short
shorts

le maillot de bain
ma-yoh duh ba(n)
swimsuit

le blouson
bloo-zo(n)
jacket

la capuche
ka-pew-sh
hood

la jupe
zhewp
skirt

l'imperméable
lam-pair-may-a-bluh
raincoat

les bottes
bot
boots

Les **jeans** et les baskets sont mes **vêtements** préférés.
Jeans and sneakers are my favorite items of **clothing**.

7

Do you like to wear sneakers?

La cuisine
Kitchen

la poêle
pwal
frying pan

l'assiette
la-see-yet
plate

le four
foor
oven

la cuisinière
kwee-zeen-yair
stove

la cuillère
kwee-yehr
spoon

la tasse
tahss
mug

le livre
lee-vruh
book

le torchon
tor-sho(n)
dish towel

le bol
bol
bowl

la casserole
kass-rol
saucepan

8

Merci de **faire la vaisselle**.
Thanks for **doing the dishes**.

le placard
plah-kar
cupboard

l'évier
leh-vyay
sink

le congélateur
kon-zhey-la-tuhr
freezer

le réfrigérateur
re-free-zhay-ra-tuhr
refrigerator

Extra words to learn

la balai
ba-lay
broom

la bouilloire
booy-wahr
kettle

la cruche
krewsh
jug

le grille-pain
gree-ye pa(n)
toaster

la machine à laver
ma-sheen ah la-vay
washing machine

le plateau
pla-toh
tray

la poubelle
poo-bell
trash can

le table
tab-luh
table

le couteau
koo-toh
knife

la fourchette
foor-shet
fork

Aimes-tu **faire des gâteaux**?
Do you like **baking**?

le tablier
tab-lee-yay
apron

le gant de cuisine
gah(n) duh kwee-zeen
oven mitt

le verre
vair
glass

9

What is on the table?

La salle de bains
Bathroom

le peigne
pain-ye
comb

la baignoire
bayn-wahr
bath

C'est rigolo de faire des **bulles**.
It's fun to make **bubbles**.

l'eau
loh
water

le jouet
zhoo-way
toy

Je mets du **dentifrice** sur ma **brosse à dents**.
I put **toothpaste** on my **toothbrush**.

l'éponge
lay-ponzh
sponge

les serviettes
sair-vee-et
towels

le tube
tewb
tube

le dentifrice
dahn-tee-freess
toothpaste

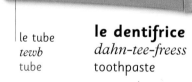

la brosse à dents
bros ah dah(n)
toothbrush

Combien d'objets jaunes y a-t-il sur cette page ?

la douche
doosh
shower

le shampooing
shahm-pwa(n)
shampoo

le miroir
meer-wahr
mirror

le papier toilette
pap-yay twa-let
toilet paper

le savon
sa-vo(n)
soap

Extra words to learn

la brosse à cheveux
bros ah shuh-vuh
hairbrush

la buée
bway
steam

le maquillage
ma-kee-yazh
makeup

les mouchoirs en papier
moosh-wahrs ah(n) pap-yay
tissues

se laver
suh la-vay
to wash oneself

la serviette de toilette
sair-vee-et duh twa-let
washcloth

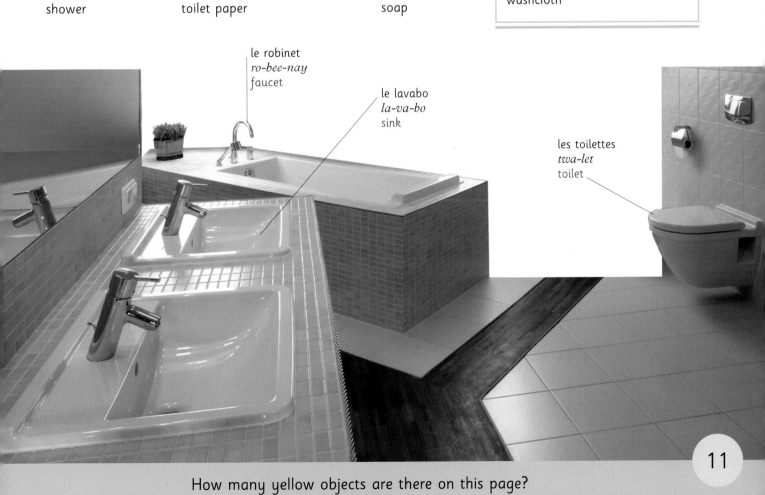

le robinet
ro-bee-nay
faucet

le lavabo
la-va-bo
sink

les toilettes
twa-let
toilet

11

How many yellow objects are there on this page?

Ma chambre
My bedroom

le réveil
ray-vaye
alarm clock

le lit
lee
bed

l'oreiller
lo-ray-yay
pillow

la couette
koo-et
comforter

la chaise
shehz
chair

la commode
kom-mod
chest of drawers

Je **dors** dans mon **lit**.
I **sleep** in my **bed**.

le jeu électronique
zhuh ay-lek-tro-neek
video game

Nous **jouons** à un jeu de société.
We are **playing** a board game.

Mon **chat** dort sous **mon lit**.
My **cat** sleeps under **my bed**.

le tapis
ta-pee
rug

la moquette
moh-ket
carpet

12

A quelle heure tu te réveilles ?

Qu'y a-t-il dans l'**armoire** ?
What is in the **wardrobe**?

les livres
leev-ruh
books

Je sais jouer de la **guitare**.
I can play the guitar.

les **échecs**
ay-shek
chess

La **moquette** est bleue.
The **carpet** is blue.

l'armoire
larm-wahr
wardrobe

la guitare
ghee-tar
guitar

le cintre
san-truh
coat hanger

la lampe
lahmp
lamp

le miroir
meer-wahr
mirror

13

Le jardin
Garden

la brouette
broo-et
wheelbarrow

l'arbre
lar-bruh
tree

le tronc
tro(n)
trunk

le râteau
rah-toh
rake

le banc
bah(n)
bench

l'herbe
lairb
grass

la tondeuse à gazon
ton-duhz ah gah-zo(n)
lawnmower

Extra words to learn

l'arrosoir
lar-rohz-wahr
watering can

la barrière
bar-yair
fence

le bulbe
bewlb
bulb

le déplantoir
day-plahnt-wahr
trowel

la feuille
fuh-ye
leaf

le jardinier
zhar-deen-yay
gardener

la pelouse
puh-looz
lawn

la serre
sair
greenhouse

De quelle couleur est la coccinelle sur cette page ?

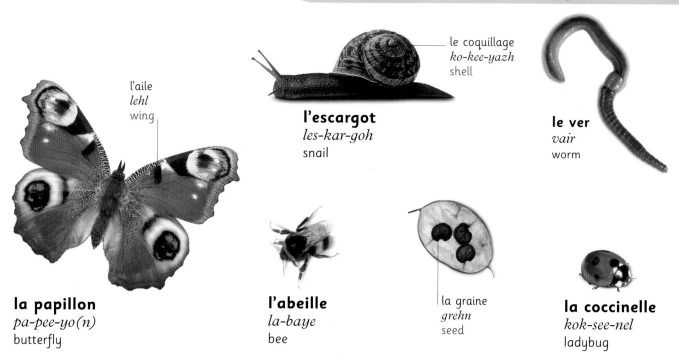

l'aile
lehl
wing

le coquillage
ko-kee-yazh
shell

l'escargot
les-kar-goh
snail

le ver
vair
worm

la papillon
pa-pee-yo(n)
butterfly

l'abeille
la-baye
bee

la graine
grehn
seed

la coccinelle
kok-see-nel
ladybug

Les **fleurs poussent** dans le **jardin**.
Flowers are **growing** in the **garden**.

Marie **creuse** dans le **jardin**.
Marie is **digging** in the **garden**.

la chenille
shuh-nee-ye
caterpillar

la fleur
fluhr
flower

la pelle
pel
shovel

la terre
tair
soil

15

What color is the ladybug on this page?

La vie en ville
City life

la maison
may-zo(n)
house

l'autobus
lohto-bews
bus

le gratte-ciel
grat syel
skyscraper

Les **villes** ont de **hauts bâtiments** appelés **gratte-ciel**.
Cities have **tall buildings** called **skyscrapers**.

l'horloge
lor-lozh
clock

la rue
rew
street

les appartements
ap-par-tuh-mah(n)
apartments

le magasin
ma-ga-za(n)
store

Quelle heure est-il sur l'horloge bleue ?

Extra words to learn

l'arrêt de bus
lar-reh duh bews
bus stop

l'autoroute
loh-toh-root
highway

la banque
bahnk
bank

le café
ka-fay
café

la gare
gar
station

la route
root
road

le trottoir
trot-wahr
sidewalk

l'usine
lew-zeen
factory

le cône de signalisation
kohn duh see-nya-lee-za-syo(n)
traffic cone

le panneau
pan-noh
sign

le cinéma
see-nay-ma
cinema

les feux de signalisation
fuh duh see-nya-lee-za-syo(n)
traffic lights

— **le réverbère**
ray-vair-bair
lamppost

le carrefour
kar-foor
intersection

le taxi
tak-see
taxi

l'hôtel
lo-tel
hotel

What is the time on the blue clock?

Au parc
In the park

le cerf-volant
sair vo-lah(n)
kite

la corde à sauter
kord ah soh-tay
jump rope

le skate-board
skate board
skateboard

les fleurs
fluhr
flowers

le tourniquet
toor-nee-kay
merry-go-round

J'adore **sauter à la corde** !
I love **jumping rope**!

As-tu un cerf-volant ?
Do you have a kite?

la fille
fee-ye
girl

18

l'arbre
lar-bruh
tree

Les **oiseaux** volent.
The **birds** are flying.

la balançoire
ba-lahn-swahr
swing

le papillon
pa-pee-yo(n)
butterfly

l'oiseau
lwa-zoh
bird

le vélo
vay-lo
bicycle

la feuille
fuh-ye
leaf

l'herbe
lairb
grass

Trois **enfants jouent** sur le **tourniquet**.
Three **children** are **playing** on the **merry-go-round**.

le garçon
gar-so(n)
boy

Mon **jeu** préféré est le **football**.
My favorite game is soccer.

**le ballon
de football**
*ba-lo(n) duh
foot-bohl*
soccer ball

Can you skateboard?

Les loisirs
Hobbies

Mes **fleurs** poussent.
My **flowers** are growing.

le jardinage
zhar-dee-nazh
gardening

faire du camping
fair dew kahm-peeng
to go camping

Je suis **prête** à aller **nager**.
I'm **ready** to go **swimming**.

la natation
na-ta-syo(n)
swimming

Mathilde **s'entraîne** tous les jours.
Mathilde **practices** every day.

jouer d'un instrument
zhoo-ay dan an-strew-mah(n)
to play an instrument

observer les oiseaux
ob-zair-vay layz wa-zoh
to go bird-watching

faire de la danse
fair duh la dahnss
to dance

Quel est ton loisir préféré ?

Extra words to learn

le chant
shah(n)
singing

collectionner
kol-lek-syo-nay
to collect

le dessin
de-sa(n)
drawing

faire la cuisine
fair la kwee-zeen
to cook

faire du roller
fair dew ro-lair
to rollerblade

faire du théâtre
fair dew tay-a-truh
to act

faire du vélo
fair dew vay-lo
to ride a bike

la lecture
lek-tewr
reading

le surf
surf
surfing

*Je **saute** et je **m'étire** à la gymnastique.*
I **jump** and **stretch** in gymnastics.

la gymnastique
zheem-nas-teek
gymnastics

prendre une photo
prahn-druh ewn fo-toh
to take a photo

la peinture
pan-tewr
painting

l'écriture
lay-kree-tewr
writing

What is your favorite hobby?

La nourriture
Food

la graine
grehn
seed

la peau
poh
peel

l'orange
lo-ranzh
orange

la pomme
pom
apple

la pastèque
pas-tehk
watermelon

la banane
ba-nan
banana

la tomate
tom-at
tomato

la carotte
ka-rot
carrot

la laitue
lay-tew
lettuce

le chou
shoo
cabbage

Nous **mangeons** des **pâtes** !
We are **eating pasta**!

le poivre
pwa-vruh
pepper

l'assiette
la-syet
plate

la salade
sal-ad
salad

la chaise
shehz
chair

le sel
sel
salt

la table
tab-luh
table

L'ananas est un **fruit**.
Pineapple is a **fruit**.

l'ananas
lah-na-nass
pineapple

Que manges-tu au petit-déjeuner ?

la pomme de terre
pom duh tair
potato

l'œuf
luhf
egg

le yaourt
ya-oort
yogurt

le lait
lay
milk

la confiture
kon-fee-tewr
jam

le beurre
buhr
butter

le pain
pa(n)
bread

J'aime le **pain** avec du **miel**.
I like **bread** with **honey**.

le miel
myel
honey

le riz
ree
rice

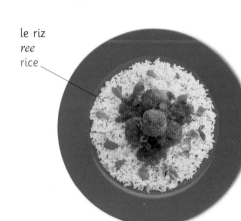

les pâtes
paht
pasta

la viande
vyahnd
meat

Extra words to learn

le biscuit
bee-skwee
cookie

la farine
fah-reen
flour

les fraises
frehz
strawberries

le fruit
frwee
fruit

le légume
lay-gewm
vegetable

l'oignon
loh-nyo(n)
onion

le poisson
pwa-so(n)
fish

le poulet
poo-lay
chicken

le sucre
soo-kruh
sugar

23

What do you eat for breakfast?

Les courses
Shopping

le prix
pree
price

le marché
mar-shay
market

l'argent
lar-zhah(n)
money

le sac
sak
shopping bag

Je **dois acheter** des **œufs**.
I **have to buy eggs**.

Nous **attendons** dans la **queue**.
We are **waiting** in **line**.

le caddie
ka-dee
shopping cart

le panier
pan-yay
basket

Aimes-tu faire les courses ?

pain
œufs
lait
beurre
sucre
farine

la liste de courses
leest duh koorss
shopping list

le supermarché
soo-pair-mar-shay
supermarket

le café
ka-fay
café

la serveuse
sair-vuhz
waitress

…e a beaucoup de **sacs** !
She has a lot of **bags**!

la boulangerie
boo-lahn-zhree
bakery

la librairie
lee-breh-ree
bookstore

les courses
koorss
shopping

Extra words to learn

l'addition
lad-dee-syo(n)
bill

la caisse
kehss
checkout, cash register

en espèces
ah(n) es-pehss
(in) cash

faire les courses
fair lay koorss
to go shopping

le magasin
ma-ga-za(n)
store

le porte-monnaie
port mo-nay
wallet, purse

le ticket de caisse
tee-kay duh kess
receipt

le vendeur
vahn-duhr
salesclerk

25

Do you like to go shopping?

À la fête
At the party

la boisson
bwa-so(n)
drink

les sandwichs
sahnd-weetsh
sandwiches

les cartes d'anniversaire
kart dah-nee-vair-sair
birthday cards

les bougies
boo-zhee
candles

le gâteau d'anniversaire
gah-toh dah-nee-vair-sair
birthday cake

C'est rigolo de **jouer** avec les **ballons**.
It's fun **to play** with **balloons**.

le magicien
ma-zhee-sya(n)
magician

Vois-tu le **gâteau d'anniversaire** ?
Can you see the **birthday cake**?

26

Tu aimes danser ?

les décorations
day-ko-ra-syo(n)
decorations

Bon anniversaire !
Happy birthday!

Je veux **ouvrir** les **cadeaux** !
I want to **open** the **presents!**

les cadeaux
ka-doh
presents

les hauts-parleurs
oh par-lur
speakers

les ballons
ba-lo(n)
balloons

l'appareil photo
lap-pa-ray fo-toh
camera

les biscuits
bee-skwee
cookies

la glace
glass
ice cream

les bonbons
bo(n)-bo(n)
candy

27

Do you like to dance?

Temps libre
Free time

l'ordinateur portable
lor-dee-na-tuhr por-tab-luh
laptop

les dés
day
dice

le robot
ro-boh
robot

le ballon
ba-lo(n)
ball

le jeu de société
zhuh duh so-see-ye-tay
board game

Je **joue** au petit **train**.
I **play** with my **train** set.

le dessin
de-sa(n)
drawing

le crayon de couleur
kra-yo(n) duh koo-luhr
colored pencil

le puzzle
puh-zluh
puzzle

le train
tra(n)
train

Aimes-tu les jeux électroniques ?

les cartes
kart
cards

le déguisement
day-gheez-mah(n)
costume

le lecteur MP3
lek-tur em-peh-trwa
MP3 player

le jeu électronique
zhuh ay-lek-tro-neek
video game

le casque
kask
helmet

Il **bouge** très vite !
He **moves** very fast!

faire du roller
fair dew ro-lur
to rollerblade

J'adore le **toboggan aquatique**.
I love the **waterslide**.

le toboggan aquatique
to-bo-ga(n) a-kwa-tik
waterslide

le cinéma
see-nay-ma
cinema

la fête foraine
fet fo-ren
amusement park

Do you like video games?

Les moyens de transport
Transportation

l'avion
lav-yo(n)
airplane

le ferry
fay-ree
ferry

le bateau à voile
ba-toh ah vwal
sailboat

le taxi
tak-see
taxi

le camion
kam-yo(n)
truck

le vélo
vay-lo
bicycle

Les **gens** voyagent en **autobus**.
People travel on the **bus**.

l'autobus
lohto-bews
bus

Pour les secours
To the rescue

le camion de pompier
kam-yo(n) duh pomp-yay
fire truck

l'échelle
ley-shell
ladder

le pneu
puh-nuh
tire

Combien de roues y a-t-il sur cette page ?

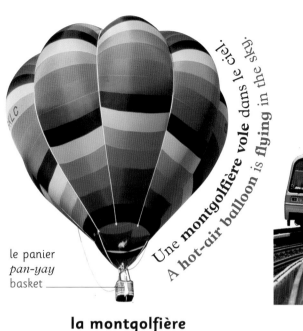

*Une **montgolfière** vole dans le ciel.*
*A **hot-air balloon** is flying in the sky.*

le panier
pan-yay
basket

la montgolfière
mohn-golf-yair
hot-air balloon

le train
tra(n)
train

Extra words to learn

l'autocar
lohto-kar
bus

le billet
bee-yay
ticket

la camionnette
kam-yon-net
van

le carburant
kar-bew-rah(n)
fuel

la fusée
few-zay
rocket ship

le garage
gar-azh
garage

l'horaire
lor-air
timetable

le voyage
vwa-yazh
journey

les bagages
bag-azh
luggage

la voiture
vwah-tewr
car

le miroir
meer-wahr
mirror

la roue
roo
wheel

la moto
moh-toh
motorcycle

l'hélicoptère de police
lay-lee-kop-tair duh po-leess
police helicopter

la voiture de police
vwa-tewr duh po-leess
police car

l'ambulance
lahm-bew-lahnss
ambulance

How many wheels are there on this page?

Les animaux de la jungle
Jungle animals

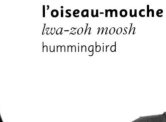

l'oiseau-mouche
lwa-zoh moosh
hummingbird

l'aile
lehl
wing

la chauve-souris
shohv soo-ree
bat

le papillon
pa-pee-yo(n)
butterfly

le chimpanzé
shahm-pahn-zay
chimpanzee

la fourmi
foor-mee
ant

l'araignée
lah-rey-nyay
spider

le gorille
go-ree-ye
gorilla

le papillon de nuit
pa-pee-yo(n) duh nwee
moth

le crocodile
kro-ko-deel
crocodile

Quels animaux peuvent voler sur cette page ?

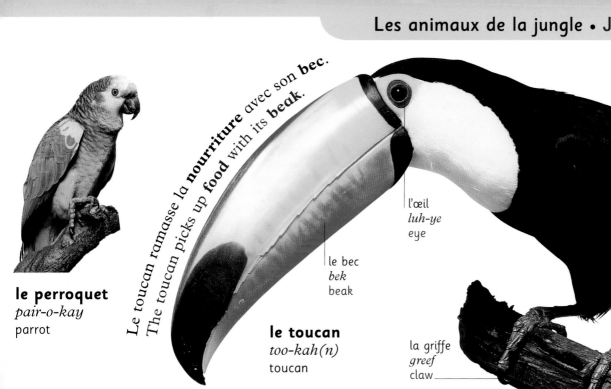

le perroquet
pair-o-kay
parrot

Le toucan ramasse la **nourriture** avec son **bec**.
The toucan picks up **food** with its **beak**.

l'œil
luh-ye
eye

le bec
bek
beak

le toucan
too-kah(n)
toucan

la griffe
greef
claw

Extra words to learn

l'aigle
lay-gluh
eagle

la forêt tropicale
for-eh tro-pee-kal
rain forest

l'insecte
lan-sekt
insect

le lézard
lay-zar
lizard

le mammifère
ma-mee-fair
mammal

l'oiseau
lwa-zoh
bird

le scarabée
ska-ra-bay
beetle

le singe
sanzh
monkey

le serpent
sair-pah(n)
snake

la grenouille
gruh-noo-ye
frog

la patte
pat
foot

les taches
tash
spots

les rayures
rey-yewr
stripes

le tigre
tee-gruh
tiger

le léopard
lay-o-par
leopard

33

Which animals on this page can fly?

Les animaux du monde
World animals

le bec
bek
beak

le manchot
mahn-shoh
penguin

le koala
ko-a-la
koala

le cerf
sair
deer

la patte
pat
paw

le lion
lee-yo(n)
lion

le panda
pahn-da
panda

La **girafe** a un long **cou** !
The **giraffe** has a long **neck!**

la girafe
zhee-raf
giraffe

l'ours blanc
loorss blah(n)
polar bear

Extra words to learn

l'alligator
lal-ee-gah-tor
alligator

le babouin
ba-bwa(n)
baboon

la hibou
ee-boo
owl

le faucon
foh-ko(n)
hawk

le loup
loo
wolf

le pélican
peh-lee-ka(n)
pelican

le renard
ruh-nar
fox

la tortue de mer
tor-tew duh mair
turtle

Combien d'oiseaux y a-t-il sur cette page ?

L'**éléphant ramasse** la **nourriture** avec sa **trompe**.
The **elephant picks up food** with its **trunk**.

le chameau
sha-moh
camel

le zèbre
zeh-bruh
zebra

les rayures
rey-yewr
stripes

la trompe
tromp
trunk

l'éléphant
lay-lay-fah(n)
elephant

l'ours
loorss
bear

le kangourou
kahn-goo-roo
kangaroo

la queue
kuh
tail

la griffe
greef
claw

le dauphin
doh-fa(n)
dolphin

la palme
pahlm
flipper

le rhinocéros
ree-no-say-ros
rhinoceros

35

How many birds are there on this page?

À la ferme
On the farm

La **fermière** **utilise** le **tracteur**.
The **farmer** **uses** the **tractor**.

la fermière
fairm-yair
farmer

le tracteur
trak-tuhr
tractor

le chien de berger
shya(n) duh bair-zhay
sheepdog

le champ
shah(m)
field

le blé
blay
wheat

les agneaux
an-yoh
lambs

le mouton
moo-to(n)
sheep

Tu sais faire du cheval ?

la moissonneuse-batteuse
mwa-son-nuhz bat-tuhz
combine harvester

la barrière
bar-yair
fence

La **vache** mange l'**herbe** dans le **champ**.
The **cow** eats the **grass** in the **field**.

Le **cheval** est **marron** et **blanc**.
The **horse** is **brown** and **white**.

le canard
ka-nar
duck

le veau
voh
calf

Le **poussin** est **près de** sa **mère**.
The **chick** is **close to** its **mother**.

la vache
vash
cow

le foin
fwa(n)
hay

le cheval
shuh-val
horse

le poulet
poo-lay
chicken

les canetons
ka-nuh-to(n)
ducklings

37

L'océan
Ocean

le bateau de pêche
ba-toh duh pehsh
fishing boat

la mouette
moo-wet
seagull

La voile est blanche.
The **sail** is white.

la voile
vwal
sail

la corde
kord
rope

le bateau à voile
ba-toh ah vwal
sailboat

le marin
mar-a(n)
sailor

Extra words to learn

l'ancre
lahn-kruh
anchor

la bouée
boo-way
buoy

le canot
kanoh
rowboat

la mer
mair
sea

la pêche
pehsh
fishing

le port
por
harbor

la vague
vahg
wave

la baleine
ba-len
whale

La baleine nage dans la **mer**.
The **whale** is swimming in the sea.

la méduse
may-dewz
jellyfish

De quelle couleur est le sous-marin ?

l'épuisette
lay-pwee-zet
net

le navire
na-veer
ship

le phare
far
lighthouse

le bateau de sauvetage
ba-toh duh sohv-tazh
lifeboat

la nageoire
na-zhwar
fin

le poisson
pwa-so(n)
fish

Un **requin** a beaucoup de **dents**.
A **shark** has lots of **teeth**.

le requin
ruh-ka(n)
shark

l'algue
lal-guh
seaweed

le sous-marin
soo ma-ra(n)
submarine

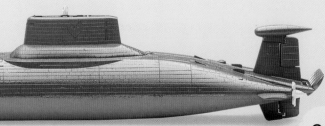

What color is the submarine?

La nature
Nature

Les nénuphars poussent dans l'eau.
Water lilies grow in water.

le bec
bek
beak

la libellule
lee-beh-lewl
dragonfly

le nénuphar
nay-new-far
water lily

le canard
ka-nar
duck

Beaucoup d'animaux vivent près des étangs.
Many animals live close to ponds.

la plante
plahnt
plant

le cygne
seen-ye
swan

le crapaud
kra-poh
toad

Combien de nénuphars y a-t-il dans l'étang ?

le nid
nee
nest

Les **têtards nagent** dans les **étangs**.
Tadpoles swim in **ponds**.

les têtards
teh-tar
tadpoles

l'antenne
lan-ten
antenna

la guêpe
gehp
wasp

l'aile
lehl
wing

la mouche
moosh
fly

le hibou
ee-boo
owl

la grenouille
gruh-noo-ye
frog

l'étang
lay-tah(n)
pond

Extra words to learn

l'eau
loh
water

la fourmi
foor-mee
ant

l'habitat
la-bee-ta
habitat

le héron
air-o(n)
heron

l'insecte
lan-sekt
insect

le lapin
la-pah(n)
rabbit

la mauvaise herbe
moh-vayz airb
weed

l'oiseau
lwa-zoh
bird

41

How many water lilies are there in the pond?

À la plage
At the beach

le seau
soh
bucket

l'algue
lal-guh
seaweed

le crabe
krab
crab

le coquillage
ko-kee-yazh
shell

les galets
ga-lay
pebbles

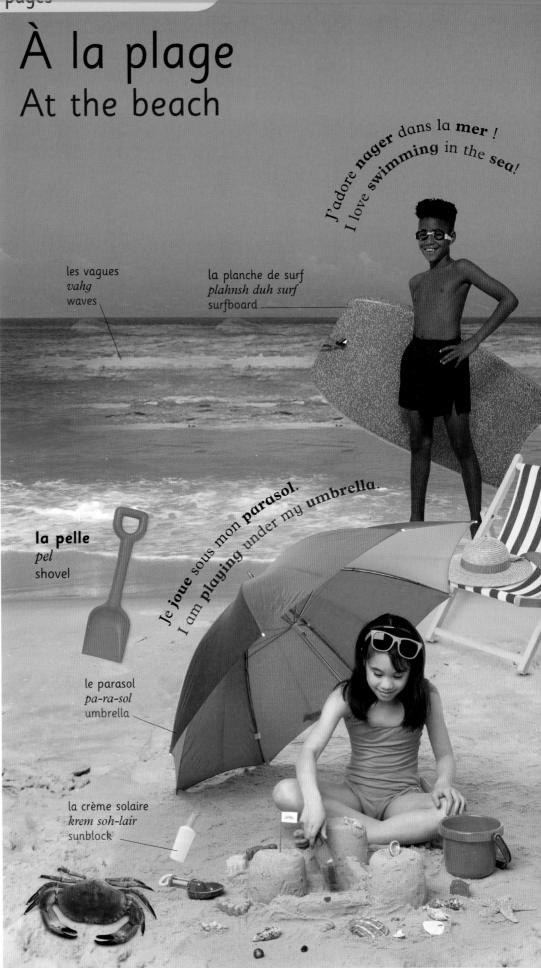

J'adore **nager** dans la **mer** !
I love **swimming** in the sea!

les vagues
vahg
waves

la planche de surf
plahnsh duh surf
surfboard

la pelle
pel
shovel

Je **joue** sous mon **parasol**.
I am **playing** under my umbrella.

le parasol
pa-ra-sol
umbrella

la crème solaire
krem soh-lair
sunblock

Aimes tu aller à la plage ?

les mouettes
moo-wet
seagulls

le maillot de bain
ma-yoh duh ba(n)
swimsuit

le rocher
ro-shay
rock

l'étoile de mer
lay-twal duh mair
starfish

la glace
glass
ice cream

J'aime m'allonger au **soleil**.
I like to lie in the **sun**.

les lunettes de natation
lew-net duh na-ta-syo(n)
goggles

le chapeau
sha-poh
sun hat

la chaise longue
shehz long-uh
deck chair

le sable
sah-bluh
sand

le château de sable
sha-toh duh sah-bluh
sandcastle

Do you like to go to the beach?

L'école
School

les ciseaux
see-zoh
scissors

les crayons de couleur
kra-yo(n) duh koo-luhr
colored pencils

le tableau noir
tab-loh nwahr
blackboard

la règle
reh-gluh
ruler

la gomme
gom
eraser

le crayon à papier
kray-o(n) ah pap-yay
pencil

le stylo
stee-loh
pen

le carnet
kar-ney
notebook

le bureau
bew-roh
desk

Extra words to learn

l'alphabet
lal-fa-bay
alphabet

la chaise
shehz
chair

le dessin
de-sa(n)
drawing

l'écriture
lay-kree-tewr
writing

la lecture
lek-tewr
reading

le maître
meh-truh
teacher (elementary school)

la salle de classe
sal duh klahss
classroom

les sciences
see-yahnss
science

Combien de livres y a-t-il sur cette page ?

Vois-tu la **pomme** dans la **boîte à déjeuner** ?
Can you see the **apple** in the **lunch box**?

la boîte à déjeuner
bwat a deh-juh-neh
lunch box

le cahier
ka-yay
notebook

le cartable
kar-ta-bluh
school bag

les feutres
fuh-truh
markers

Trouve ton **pays** sur le **globe**.
Find your **country** on the **globe**.

le globe
glob
globe

l'ordinateur
lor-dee-na-tuhr
computer

les livres
lee-vruh
books

l'uniforme scolaire
lew-nee-form sko-lair
school uniform

45

How many books can you see on this page?

Les sports
Sports

Je porte un **casque**.
I am wearing a **helmet**.

le casque
kask
helmet

le ski
skee
skiing

les skis
skee
skis

la raquette
ra-ket
racket

faire du vélo
fair dew vay-lo
to ride a bike

la roue
roo
wheel

le patinage sur glace
pa-tee-nazh soor glass
ice-skating

la gymnastique
zheem-nas-teek
gymnastics

Nous **jouons** au **basket-ball**.
We are **playing basketball**.

Delphine **veut** marquer un **but**.
Delphine **wants** to score a **goal**.

le tee-shirt
tee shirt
T-shirt

le short
short
shorts

le football
foot-bohl
soccer

les baskets
bas-ket
sneakers

le basket-ball
basket bohl
basketball

le golf
golf
golf

Aimes-tu faire du sport ?

Extra words to learn

l'athlétisme
lat-lay-tee-smah
athletics

le base-ball
bayz bohl
baseball

l'exercice
lek-sair-seess
exercise

le hockey
oh-kay
hockey

le hockey sur glace
oh-kay soor glass
ice hockey

le judo
zhew-doh
judo

le karaté
ka-ra-tay
karate

la natation
na-ta-syo(n)
swimming

la voile
vwal
sail

le gilet de sauvetage
zhee-leh duh so-vuh-tazh
life jacket

la plongée
plon-zhay
diving

faire de la voile
fair duh la vwal
to sail

la balle
bahl
ball

le gant
gah(n)
glove

la rame
rahm
oar

*Je **tire** sur les **rames**.*
I **pull** on the **oars**.

faire de l'aviron
fair duh la-vee-ron
to row

le bateau
ba-toh
boat

la batte
bat
bat

le cheval
shuh-val
horse

l'équitation
lay-kee-ta-syo(n)
horseback riding

le rugby
rewg-bee
rugby

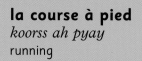

la course à pied
koorss ah pyay
running

le tennis
ten-neess
tennis

47

Do you like to play sports?

Les animaux domestiques
Pets

Mon **chiot** s'appelle Toby.
My **puppy** is called Toby.

le chiot
shyoh
puppy

bol
bol
bowl

la nourriture
noo-ree-tewr
food

le cochon d'Inde
ko-sho(n) dand
guinea pig

Une **tortue** bouge très **lentement**.
A **tortoise** moves very slowly.

la tortue
tor-tew
tortoise

le hamster
am-stair
hamster

le lapin
la-pah(n)
rabbit

le chat
sha
cat

le poisson rouge
pwa-so(n) roozh
goldfish

De quelle couleur sont les poils du cochon d'Inde ?

les poils
pwal
hair

la langue
lahng
tongue

le chaton
sha-to(n)
kitten

le chien
shya(n)
dog

Un **perroquet** a des **plumes** de toutes les **couleurs**.
A **parrot** has **feathers** of all **colors**.

le bec
bek
beak

le perroquet
pair-o-kay
parrot

Paul brosse le **cheval**.
Paul brushes the **horse**.

l'oiseau
lwa-zoh
bird

la queue
kuh
tail

les moustaches
moose-tash
whiskers

la souris
soo-ree
mouse

le cheval
shuh-val
horse

49

What color is the guinea pig's hair?

Les couleurs et les formes
Colors and shapes

rouge
roozh
red

orange
o-ranzh
orange

jaune
zhohn
yellow

vert
vair
green

bleu
bluh
blue

violet
vyo-lay
purple

rose
rohz
pink

marron
mar-o(n)
brown

noir
nwahr
black

courbé
koor-beh
curved

droit
drwa
straight

Quelle est ta couleur préférée ?

le carré
kar-ray
square

le cercle
sair-kluh
circle

l'arc-en-ciel
lark en see-yel
rainbow

le triangle
tree-yahn-gluh
triangle

l'étoile
lay-twal
star

le losange
lo-zahnzh
diamond

le rectangle
rek-tahn-gluh
rectangle

l'hexagone
exa-gone
hexagon

le pentagone
pa(n)-ta-gone
pentagon

le cube
kewb
cube

la sphère
sfair
sphere

Extra words to learn

blanc
blah(n)
white

clair
klair
light (not dark)

coloré
ko-lo-ray
colorful

le cœur
kuhr
heart

gris
gree
gray

l'ovale
lo-val
oval

rond
ro(n)
round

sombre
som-bruh
dark

51

What is your favorite color?

Les contraires
Opposites

Ouvre **grand** !
Open **wide**!

rugueux
rew-ghuh
rough

lisse
leess
smooth

ouvert
oo-vair
open

mouillé
moo-yay
wet

sec
sek
dry

fermé
fair-may
closed

sale
sal
dirty

propre
prop-ruh
clean

Extra words to learn

léger
lay-zhay
light (weight)

lent
lah(n)
slow

lourd
loor
heavy

nouveau
noo-voh
new

plein
pla(n)
full

rapide
ra-peed
fast

vide
veed
empty

vieux
vyuh
old

Préfères-tu les boissons chaudes ou froides ?

Une **citrouille** devient **grosse** en **automne**.
A **pumpkin** gets **fat** in the **autumn**.

froid
frwa
cold

chaud
shoh
hot

Ce **légume** est très **fin**.
This **vegetable** is very **thin**.

gros
groh
fat/big

fin
fa(n)
thin

doux
doo
soft

dur
dewr
hard

Le tournesol a une **grande** tige.
Sunflowers have **tall** stems.

Cette fleur a une tige **courte**.
This flower has a **short** stem.

grand
grah(n)
tall

court
koor
short

petit
puh-tee
small

grand
grah(n)
big

53

Do you prefer hot or cold drinks?

Le temps qu'il fait
Weather

le bonhomme de neige
bon-om duh nehzh
snowman

l'automne
loh-ton
fall

l'hiver
lee-vair
winter

les flocons de neige
flo-ko(n) duh nehzh
snowflakes

la neige
nehzh
snow

le bonnet
bon-nay
wool hat

J'ai fait un bonhomme de neige.
I built a snowman.

Je porte une écharpe et des gants.
I am wearing a scarf and gloves.

le vent
vah(n)
wind

le printemps
pran-tah(m)
spring

J'ai un **parapluie** jaune.
I have a yellow **umbrella**.

l'été
lay-tay
summer

le soleil
so-laye
sun

Il fait **chaud** au **soleil**.
It is **hot** in the **sun**.

la pluie
plwee
rain

le nuage
new-azh
cloud

l'arc-en-ciel
lark en see-yel
rainbow

les lunettes de soleil
lew-net duh so-laye
sunglasses

la casquette
kas-ket
cap

55

Aa

b
c
d
e
f
g
h
i
j
k
l
m
n
o
p
q
r
s
t
u
v
w
x
y
z

English A–Z

In this section, English words are in alphabetical order, followed by their French translations. There is information after each English word to show you what type of word it is. This will help you make sentences. In French, nouns (naming words) are either masculine (m) or feminine (f). If the French word has *un/le* before it, it is masculine; if it has *une/la*, it is feminine. Nouns that are plural have *des/les* before them. See page 113 for the pronunciation guide.

(n) = noun (a naming word). Either masculine or feminine. Feminine nouns usually have an "e" at the end.
(adj) = adjective (a describing word). These words can change depending on whether the noun they are describing is masculine (m) or feminine (f).
(adv) = adverb (a word that gives more information about a verb, an adjective, or another adverb)
(conj) = conjunction (a joining word; for example, "and")
(prep) = preposition (for example, "about")
(pron) = pronoun (for example, "he," "she," "it")
(article) = (for example, "a," "an," "the")
(sing) = singular (one thing) **(plu)** = plural (lots of things)
(m) = masculine **(f)** = feminine

apple
la pomme

a (article)
un (m) une (f)
a(n)/ewn

about (adv)
environ
ahn-vee-ron

about (prep)
sur
soor

above (prep)
au-dessus de
oh duhs-ew duh

accident (n)
un accident
ak-see-dah(n)

across (prep)
de l'autre côté de
duh loh-truh koh-tay duh

activity (n)
une activité
ak-tee-vee-tay

address (n)
une adresse
a-dress

adult (n)
un/une adulte
a-dewlt

adventure (n)
une aventure
a-vahn-tewr

after (prep)
après
ah-prey

afternoon (n)
un après-midi
ah-prey mee-dee

again (adv)
encore
ahn-kor

age (n)
l'âge (m)
lahzh

air (n)
l'air (m)
lair

airplane (n)
un avion
av-yo(n)

airport (n)
un aéroport
a-ay-ro-por

alarm clock (n)
un réveil
ray-vaye

all (adj)
tout (m) toute (f)
too/toot

alligator (n)
un alligator
ah-lee-gah-tor

almost (adv)
presque
presk

alone (adj)
seul (m) seule (f)
suhl

alphabet (n)
l'alphabet (m)
lal-fa-bay

already (adv)
déjà
day-zha

also (adv)
aussi
oh-see

always (adv)
toujours
too-zhoor

amazing (adj)
incroyable
an-krwa-ya-bluh

ambulance (n)
une ambulance
ahm-bew-lahnss

amusement park (n)
une fête foraine
fet fo-ren

an (article)
un (m) une (f)
a(n)/ewn

anchor (n)
une ancre
ahn-kruh

and (conj)
et
eh

angry (adj)
en colère
ah(n) ko-lehr

airplane
l'avion

Aa

b
c
d
e
f
g
h
i
j
k
l
m
n
o
p
q
r
s
t
u
v
w
x
y
z

animal (n)
un animal
ah-nee-mal

ankle (n)
une cheville
shuh-vee-ye

answer (n)
une réponse
ray-ponss

ant (n)
une fourmi
foor-mee

antenna (n)
une antenne
an-ten

anybody (pron)
n'importe qui
nam-port kee

anything (pron)
n'importe quoi
nam-port kwa

apartment (n)
un appartement
ap-par-tuh-mah(n)

app (n)
une appli
ap-lee

appearance (n)
une apparence
ap-par-ahnss

apple (n)
une pomme
pom

apron (n)
un tablier
ta-blee-yey

arch (n)
une arche
arsh

area (n)
une région
ray-zhyo(n)

arm (n)
un bras
bra

armchair (n)
un fauteuil
foh-tuh-ye

army (n)
une armée
ar-may

around (prep)
autour
oh-toor

arrival (n)
une arrivée
ar-ree-vay

arrow (n)
une flèche
flehsh

astronaut
l'astronaute

armchair
le fauteuil

art (n)
l'art (m)
lar

artist (n)
un/une artiste
ar-teest

assistant (n)
un assistant
a-seess-tah(n)

une assistante
a-seess-tahnt

astronaut (n)
un/une astronaute
astro-noht

astronomer (n)
un/une astronome
astro-nom

athletics (n)
l'athlétisme (m)
la-tlay-tees-muh

atlas (n)
un atlas
at-lahs

attic (n)
un grenier
gruhn-yay

aunt (n)
une tante
tahnt

autumn (n)
l'automne (m)
loh-ton

avocado (n)
un avocat
ah-vo-ka

away (adj)
absent (m)
ap-sah(n)

absente (f)
ap-sahnt

57

a

Bb

c

d

e

f

g

h

i

j

k

l

m

n

o

p

q

r

s

t

u

v

w

x

y

z

B

balloon
le ballon

baboon (n)
un babouin
ba-bwa(n)

baby (n)
un bébé
bay-bay

back (body) (n)
un dos
do

back (adv)
à l'arrière
ah lar-yehr

backpack (n)
un sac à dos
sak ah do

backward (adv)
en arrière
ah(n) ar-yehr

bad (adj)
mauvais (m)
moh-vay

mauvaise (f)
moh-vayz

badge (n)
un badge
bad-zhuh

badminton (n)
le badminton
bad-meen-ton

bag (n)
un sac
sak

bakery (n)
une boulangerie
boo-lahn-zhree

balcony (n)
un balcon
bal-ko(n)

ball (n)
une balle
bahl

un ballon
ba-lo(n)

ballet dancer (n)
un danseur classique
dahn-suhr kla-seek

une danseuse classique
dahn-suhz kla-seek

balloon (n)
un ballon
ba-lo(n)

bear
l'ours

banana (n)
une banane
ba-nan

band (music) (n)
un groupe
groop

bank (money) (n)
une banque
bahnk

bank (river) (n)
une rive
reev

barbecue (n)
un barbecue
bar-buh-kew

barn (n)
une grange
grahnzh

baseball (n)
le base-ball
bayz bohl

basket (n)
un panier
pan-yay

basketball (n)
le basket-ball
basket bohl

bat (animal) (n)
une chauve-souris
shohv soo-ree

bat (sports) (n)
une batte
bat

bath (n)
une baignoire
bayn-wahr

bathroom (n)
une salle de bains
sal duh ba(n)

battery (n)
une pile
peel

battle (n)
une bataille
ba-tah-ye

bat
la chauve-souris

beach (n)
une plage
plazh

bead (n)
une perle
pairl

beak (n)
un bec
bek

beans (green) (n)
des haricots verts (m)
ah-ree-koh vair

bear (n)
un ours
oorss

beard (n)
une barbe
barb

beautiful (adj)
beau (m) belle (f)
boh/bell

beauty (n)
la beauté
boh-tay

because (conj)
parce que
par-suh-kuh

bed (n)
un lit
lee

bedroom (n)
une chambre
shahm-bruh

bee (n)
une abeille
a-baye

beetle (n)
un scarabée
ska-ra-bay

before (prep)
avant
av-ah(n)

behind (prep)
derrière
dair-yehr

bell (n)
une cloche
klosh

below (prep)
au-dessous de
oh duh-soo duh

belt (n)
une ceinture
sehn-ture

bench (n)
un banc
bah(n)

best (adj)
mieux
myuh

better (adj)
meilleur (m)
meilleure (f)
may-yuhr

between (prep)
entre
ahn-truh

saddle
la selle

bicycle
le vélo

pedal
la pédale

wheel
la roue

tire
le pneu

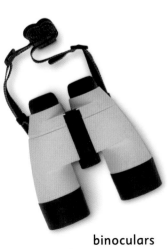

binoculars
des jumelles

bicycle (n)
un vélo
vay-lo

big (wide) (adj)
gros (m) grosse (f)
groh/grohss

big (tall) (adj)
grand (m)
grah(n)

grande (f)
grahnd

bill (n)
une addition
ad-dee-syo(n)

bill (paper money) (n)
un billet
bee-yay

billion (n)
milliard
meel-yar

binoculars (n)
des jumelles (f)
zhew-mel

bird (n)
un oiseau
wa-zoh

birthday (n)
un anniversaire
ah-nee-vair-sair

birthday cake (n)
un gâteau
d'anniversaire
gah-toh
dah-nee-vair-sair

birthday card (n)
une carte
d'anniversaire
kart dah-nee-vair-sair

black (adj)
noir (m)
noire (f)
nwahr

blackboard (n)
un tableau noir
tab-loh nwahr

blanket (n)
une couverture
koo-vair-tewr

blonde (adj)
blond (m)
bloh(n)

blonde (f)
blohnd

blood (n)
le sang
sah(n)

blouse (n)
un chemisier
shuh-meez-yay

blue (adj)
bleu (m) bleue (f)
bluh

board (sign) (n)
un panneau
pan-noh

board game (n)
un jeu de
société
zhuh duh
so-see-ye-tay

boat (n)
un bateau
ba-toh

a
Bb
c
d
e
f
g
h
i
j
k
l
m
n
o
p
q
r
s
t
u
v
w
x
y
z

Bb

a
c
d
e
f
g
h
i
j
k
l
m
n
o
p
q
r
s
t
u
v
w
x
y
z

body (n)
un corps
kor

bone (n)
un os
oss

book (n)
un livre
lee-vruh

bookstore (n)
une librairie
lee-breh-ree

boot (n)
une botte
bot

boring (adj)
ennuyeux (m)
ahn-wee-yuh

ennuyeuse (f)
ahn-wee-yuhz

boss
chef
shef

bottle (n)
une bouteille
boo-taye

bottom (base) (n)
le fond
foh(n)

bowl (cereal) (n)
un bol
bol

box (n)
une boîte
bwat

boy (n)
un garçon
gar-so(n)

boyfriend (n)
un petit ami
puh-tee-ta-mee

bracelet (n)
un bracelet
bra-slay

brain (n)
un cerveau
sair-voh

branch (n)
une branche
brahnsh

brave (adj)
courageux (m)
koo-ra-zhuh

courageuse (f)
koo-ra-zhuh(z)

bread (n)
un pain
pa(n)

break (pause) (n)
une pause
pohz

breakfast (n)
un petit-déjeuner
puh-tee day-zhuh-nay

breeze (n)
une brise
breez

bubbles
des bulles

butterfly
le papillon

bridge (n)
un pont
po(n)

bright (adj)
brillant (m)
bree-yah(n)

brillante (f)
bree-yahnt

broken (adj)
cassé (m)
cassée (f)
kah-say

broom (n)
un balai
ba-lay

brother (n)
un frère
frair

brown (adj)
marron
mar-o(n)

bubble (n)
une bulle
bewl

bucket (n)
un seau
soh

building (n)
un bâtiment
bah-tee-mah(n)

bulb (light) (n)
une ampoule
ahm-pool

bulb (plant) (n)
un bulbe
bewlb

buoy (n)
une bouée
boo-way

bus (n)
un autobus
ohto-bews

bus stop (n)
un arrêt de bus
ar-reh duh bews

bush (n)
un buisson
bwee-so(n)

business (n)
les affaires (f)
a-fair

busy (adj)
occupé (m) occupée (f)
oh-kew-peh

but (conj)
mais
may

butter (n)
le beurre
buhr

butterfly (n)
un papillon
pa-pee-yo(n)

button (n)
un bouton
boo-to(n)

C

cake
le gâteau

cabbage (n)
un chou
shoo

café (n)
un café
ka-fay

cage (n)
une cage
kahzh

cake (n)
un gâteau
gah-toh

calculator (n)
une calculatrice
kal-kew-la-treess

calendar (n)
un calendrier
kal-ahn-dree-yay

calf (n)
un veau
voh

calm (adj)
calme
kalm

camel (n)
un chameau
sha-moh

camera (n)
un appareil photo
ap-pa-ray fo-toh

can (drink) (n)
une cannette
ka-net

candle (n)
une bougie
boo-zhee

candy (n)
un bonbon
bo(n)-bo(n)

canoe (n)
un canoë
kan-o-ay

cap (n)
une casquette
kas-ket

capital (city) (n)
une capitale
ka-pee-tal

car (n)
une voiture
vwah-tewr

card (greeting) (n)
une carte
kart

cardboard (n)
le carton
kar-to(n)

cards (playing) (n)
des cartes (f)
kart

careful (adj)
prudent (m)
prew-dah(n)

prudente (f)
prew-dahnt

carpet (n)
une moquette
moh-ket

carrot (n)
une carotte
ka-rot

cart (n)
une charrette
sha-ret

(in) cash (n)
en espèces
ah(n) es-pehss

cash register (n)
une caisse
kess

cat (n)
un chat
sha

caterpillar (n)
une chenille
shuh-nee-ye

cave (n)
une grotte
grot

CD (n)
un CD
say-day

ceiling (n)
un plafond
pla-fo(n)

cellar (n)
une cave
kav

cell phone (n)
un téléphone portable/
un portable
tay-lay-fon por-ta-bluh

center (n)
le centre
sahn-truh

cereal (n)
une céréale
seh-reh-ahl

certain (adj)
certain (m)
sair-ta(n)

certaine (f)
sair-tehn

chain (n)
une chaîne
shehn

chair (n)
une chaise
shehz

challenge (n)
un défi
day-fee

change (n)
un changement
shahnzh-mah(n)

cheap (adj)
bon marché
bo(n) mar-shay

checkout (n)
une caisse
kehss

cheese (n)
un fromage
fro-mazh

car
la voiture

door
la portière

a
b
Cc
d
e
f
g
h
i
j
k
l
m
n
o
p
q
r
s
t
u
v
w
x
y
z

61

a
b

Cc

d
e
f
g
h
i
j
k
l
m
n
o
p
q
r
s
t
u
v
w
x
y
z

cheetah (n)
un guépard
gay-par

chef (n)
un/une chef
shef

chess (n)
les échecs (m)
ay-shek

chest (body) (n)
la poitrine
pwa-treen

chest of drawers (n)
une commode
kom-mod

chewing gum (n)
un chewing-gum
shweeng gom

chick (n)
un poussin
poo-sa(n)

chicken (meat) (n)
le poulet
poo-lay

child (n)
un/une enfant
ahn-fah(n)

children (n)
des enfants (m/f)
ahn-fah(n)

chocolate
le chocolat

chimney (n)
une cheminée
shuh-mee-nay

chimpanzee (n)
un chimpanzé
shahm-pahn-zay

chin (n)
un menton
mahn-to(n)

chocolate (n)
le chocolat
sho-ko-la

Christmas (n)
Noël (m)
no-el

church (n)
une église
ay-glee-z

cinema (movie theater) (n)
un cinéma
see-nay-ma

circle (n)
un cercle
sair-kluh

circus (n)
un cirque
seerk

city (n)
une ville
veel

classroom (n)
une salle de classe
sal duh klahss

claw (n)
une griffe
greef

clean (adj)
propre
prop-ruh

clear (adj)
clair (m)
claire (f)
klair

clever (adj)
intelligent (m)
an-tel-lee-zhah(n)

intelligente (f)
an-tel-lee-zhahnt

cliff (n)
une falaise
fa-lehz

cloak (n)
une cape
kap

clock (n)
une horloge
or-lozh

close (near) (prep)
proche
prosh

closed (adj)
fermé (m)
fermée (f)
fair-may

cloth (n)
un tissu
tee-soo

clothes (n)
des vêtements (m)
veht-mah(n)

cloud (n)
un nuage
new-azh

cloudy (adj)
nuageux (m)
new-azh-uh

nuageuse (f)
new-azh-uhz

clown (n)
un clown
kloon

coast (n)
une côte
koht

coat (n)
un manteau
mahn-toh

coat hanger (n)
un cintre
san-truh

coffee (n)
le café
ka-fay

coin (n)
une pièce
pyehs

cold (adj)
froid (m)
frwa

froide (f)
frwad

collar (dog)
un collier
kol-yay

color (n)
une couleur
koo-luhr

colored pencil (n)
un crayon de couleur
kra-yo(n) duh koo-luhr

colorful (adj)
coloré (m)
colorée (f)
ko-lo-ray

comb (n)
un peigne
pain-ye

compass
la boussole

combine harvester (n)
une moissonneuse-batteuse
mwa-son-nuhz bat-tuhz

comfortable (adj)
confortable
kon-for-ta-bluh

comforter (n)
une couette
koo-et

comic (book) (n)
une bande-dessinée
ban-deh-see-nay

compass (n)
une boussole
boo-sol

computer (n)
un ordinateur
or-dee-na-tuhr

concert (n)
un concert
kon-sair

crab
le crabe

continent (n)
un continent
kon-tee-nah(n)

controls (n)
des commandes (f)
ko-mahnd

cookie (n)
un biscuit
bee-skwee

cool (adj)
frais (m)
fray

fraîche (f)
frehsh

corner (n)
un coin
kwa(n)

correct (adj)
juste
zhewst

costume (n)
un costume
kos-tewm

un déguisement
day-gheez-mah(n)

cotton (n)
le coton
ko-to(n)

cough (n)
une toux
too

country (n)
un pays
pay-ee

countryside (n)
la campagne
kahm-pan-ye

cousin (n)
un cousin
koo-za(n)

une cousine
koo-zeen

cow (n)
une vache
vash

cowboy (n)
un cow-boy
koh boye

crab (n)
un crabe
krab

crane (n)
une grue
grew

crayon (n)
un crayon
de couleur
*kray-o(n)
duh koo-luhr*

cream (n)
la crème
krehm

creature (n)
une bête
beht

crew (n)
un équipage
ay-kee-pazh

crocodile (n)
un crocodile
kro-ko-deel

crop (n)
une récolte
ray-kolt

crosswalk (n)
un passage clouté
pa-sazh kloo-tay

crowded (adj)
bondé (m)
bondée (f)
bon-day

crown (n)
une couronne
koo-ron

cube (n)
un cube
kewb

cup (n)
une tasse
tahss

cupboard (n)
un placard
plah-kar

curious (adj)
curieux (m)
kew-ree-uh

curieuse (f)
kew-ree-uhz

curly (adj)
frisé (m) frisée (f)
free-zay

curtain (n)
un rideau
ree-doh

curved (adj)
courbé
koor-beh

cushion (n)
un coussin
koo-sa(n)

customer (n)
un client
klee-ah(n)

une cliente
klee-ahnt

crown
la couronne

a
b
Cc
d
e
f
g
h
i
j
k
l
m
n
o
p
q
r
s
t
u
v
w
x
y
z

63

D

a
b
c
Dd
e
f
g
h
i
j
k
l
m
n
o
p
q
r
s
t
u
v
w
x
y
z

daisy
la pâquerette

dad (n)
papa (m)
pa-pa

dairy (adj)
laitier (m) laitière (f)
layt-yay/layt-yair

daisy (n)
une pâquerette
pa-kuh-ret

dancer (n)
un danseur
dahn-suhr

une danseuse
dahn-suhz

dandelion (n)
un pissenlit
pee-sahn-lee

danger (n)
un danger
dahn-zhay

dangerous (adj)
dangereux (m)
dahn-zhay-ruh

dangereuse (f)
dahn-zhay-ruhz

dark (adj)
sombre
som-bruh

date (n)
une date
dat

daughter (n)
une fille
fee-ye

day (n)
un jour
zhoor

dead (adj)
mort (m) morte (f)
mor/mort

deaf (adj)
sourd (m) sourde (f)
soor/soord

dear (expensive, special) (adj)
cher (m) chère (f)
shair

deck (boat) (n)
un pont
po(n)

deck chair (n)
une chaise longue
shehz long-uh

decoration (n)
une décoration
day-ko-ra-syo(n)

deep (adj)
profond (m)
pro-fo(n)

profonde (f)
pro-fond

deer (n)
un cerf
sair

delicious (adj)
délicieux (m)
day-lee-syuh

délicieuse (f)
day-lee-syuhz

dentist (n)
un/une dentiste
dahn-teest

desert (n)
un désert
day-zair

desk (n)
un bureau
bew-roh

dessert (n)
un dessert
deh-sair

diagram (n)
un diagramme
dya-gram

diamond (shape) (n)
un losange
lo-zahnzh

diary (personal) (n)
un journal
zhoor-nal

dice (n)
des dés (m)
day

dictionary (n)
un dictionnaire
deek-syo-nair

different (adj)
différent (m)
dee-fay-rah(n)

différente (f)
dee-fay-rahnt

difficult (adj)
difficile
dee-fee-seel

digital (adj)
numérique
new-meh-rik

dining room (n)
une salle à manger
sal ah mahn-zhay

dinner (n)
un dîner
dee-nay

dinosaur (n)
un dinosaure
dee-noh-zor

direction (n)
une direction
dee-rek-syo(n)

directly (adv)
directement
dee-rek-tuh-mah(n)

dirty (adj)
sale
sal

disabled (adj)
handicapé (m)
handicapée (f)
ahn-dee-ka-pay

disco (nightclub) (n)
une discothèque
dee-sko-tek

(doing the) dishes (n)
la vaisselle
vay-sel

dish towel (n)
un torchon
tor-sho(n)

distance (n)
une distance
dee-stahnss

diving (n)
la plongée
plon-zhay

divorced (adj)
divorcé (m)
divorcée (f)
dee-vor-say

doctor (n)
un médecin
may-duh-sa(n)

doctor's office (n)
un cabinet médical
ka-bee-nay may-dee-kal

dog (n)
un chien
shya(n)

doll (n)
une poupée
poo-pay

dolphin (n)
un dauphin
doh-fa(n)

dome (n)
un dôme
dohm

door (n)
une porte
port

downstairs (adv)
au rez-de-chaussée
ray duh shoh-say

dragon (n)
un dragon
dra-go(n)

dragonfly (n)
une libellule
lee-beh-lewl

drawer (n)
un tiroir
teer-wahr

drawing (act of) (n)
le dessin
de-sa(n)

dream (n)
un rêve
rehv

dress (n)
une robe
rob

drink (n)
une boisson
bwa-so(n)

drop (n)
une goutte
goot

drum (n)
un tambour
tahm-boor

drum kit (n)
une batterie
bat-tree

dry (adj)
sec (m) sèche (f)
sek/sehsh

duck (n)
un canard
ka-nar

duckling (n)
un caneton
ka-nuh-to(n)

during (prep)
pendant
pahn-dah(n)

dust (n)
la poussière
poo-syair

DVD (n)
un DVD
day-vay-day

DVD player (n)
un lecteur de DVD
lek-tuhr duh day-vay-day

duck
le canard

egg
l'œuf

each (adj)
chaque
shak

eagle (n)
un aigle
ay-gluh

ear (n)
une oreille
o-raye

earache (n)
une otite
o-teet

early (adv)
tôt
toh

earring (n)
une boucle d'oreille
book-luh do-raye

Earth (planet) (n)
la Terre
tair

earthworm (n)
un ver de terre
vair duh tair

east (n)
l'est (m)
lest

easy (adj)
facile
fa-seel

echo (n)
un écho
ay-ko

edge (n)
le bord
bor

effect (n)
un effet
ay-fay

egg (n)
un œuf
uhf

elbow (n)
un coude
kood

electrical (adj)
électrique
ay-lek-treek

electronic game (n)
un jeu électronique
zhuh ay-lek-tro-neek

elephant (n)
un éléphant
ay-lay-fah(n)

elevator (n)
un ascenseur
a-sahn-suhr

email (n)
un courriel
koo-ree-yel

email address (n)
une adresse
électronique
*a-dress
ay-lek-tro-neek*

emergency (n)
une urgence
ewr-zhahnss

empty (adj)
vide
veed

a b c **Dd Ee** f g h i j k l m n o p q r s t u v w x y z

65

a
b
c
d

Ee

f
g
h
i
j
k
l
m
n
o
p
q
r
s
t
u
v
w
x
y
z

encyclopedia (n)
une encyclopédie
ahn-see-klo-pay-dee

end (final part) (n)
la fin
fa(n)

English (n)
l'anglais (m)
lahn-glay

enough (adj)
assez
ah-say

enthusiastic (adj)
enthousiaste
ahn-too-zee-ast

entrance (n)
une entrée
ahn-tray

envelope (n)
une enveloppe
ahn-vlop

environment (n)
un environnement
ahn-vee-ron-mah(n)

equal (adj)
égal (m) égale (f)
ay-gal

equator (n)
l'équateur (m)
lay-kwa-tuhr

equipment (n)
le matériel
ma-tay-ree-el

eraser (n)
une gomme
gom

even (adv)
même
mehm

stamp
le timbre

Tour Eiffel
Champ-de-Mars
75007 Paris
FRANCE

envelope
l'enveloppe

address
l'adresse

evening (n)
un soir
swahr

event (n)
un événement
ay-vayn-mah(n)

every (adj)
tous
too

every day (adv)
tous les jours
too lay zhoor

everybody (pron)
tout le monde
too luh mond

everything (pron)
tout
too

everywhere (adv)
partout
par-too

exam (n)
un examen
eg-za-ma(n)

excellent (adj)
excellent (m)
ek-say-lah(n)

excellente (f)
ek-say-lahnt

exchange (n)
un échange
ay-shahnzh

excited (adj)
excité (m)
excitée (f)
ek-see-tay

exercise (n)
un exercice
ek-sair-seess

exit (n)
la sortie
sor-tee

expedition (n)
une expédition
ek-spay-dee-syo(n)

expensive (adj)
cher (m) chère (f)
shair

experiment (n)
une expérience
ek-spay-ree-ahnss

expert (n)
un expert
ek-spair

une experte
ek-spairt

explorer (n)
un explorateur
ek-splor-a-tuhr

une exploratrice
ek-splor-a-treess

explosion (n)
une explosion
ek-sploh-zyo(n)

extinct (adj)
éteint (m)
ay-ta(n)

éteinte (f)
ay-tant

extra (adj)
supplémentaire
soo-play-mahn-tair

extremely (adv)
extrêmement
ek-streh-muh-mah(n)

eye (n)
un œil
uh-ye

eyebrow (n)
un sourcil
soor-seel

eyelash (n)
un cil
seel

arm
le bras

exercise
l'exercice

hand
la main

leg
la jambe

foot
le pied

F

costume
le déguisement

fabulous (adj)
fabuleux (m)
fa-bew-luh

fabuleuse (f)
fa-bew-luhz

face (n)
un visage
vee-zazh

fact (n)
un fait
fay

factory (n)
une usine
ew-zeen

faint (pale) (adj)
faible
fay-bluh

fair (n)
une foire
fwahr

false (adj)
faux (m)
fausse (f)
foh/fohss

family (n)
une famille
fa-mee-ye

famous (adj)
célèbre
say-lay-bruh

fantastic (adj)
fantastique
fan-tas-teek

far (adv)
loin
lwa(n)

farm (n)
une ferme
fairm

farmer (n)
un fermier
fairm-yay

une fermière
fairm-yair

fashion (n)
la mode
mod

fashionable (adj)
à la mode
ah la mod

fast (adv)
rapide
ra-peed

fat (adj)
gros (m)
grosse (f)
groh/grohss

father (n)
un père
pair

faucet (n)
un robinet
ro-bee-nay

favorite (adj)
préféré (m)
préférée (f)
pray-fair-ay

feather (n)
une plume
plewm

female (human) (n)
une femme
fam

fence (n)
une barrière
bar-yair

ferry (n)
un ferry
fay-ree

festival (n)
une fête
feht

field (n)
un champ
shah(m)

film (n)
un film
feelm

fin (n)
une nageoire
na-zhwar

fine (adv)
bien
bya(n)

finger (n)
un doigt
dwa

fire (n)
un feu
fuh

fire truck (n)
un camion
de pompier
*kam-yo(n)
duh pomp-yay*

firefighter (n)
un pompier
pomp-yay

first (adv)
d'abord
da-bor

first (adj)
premier (m)
pruhm-yay

première (f)
pruhm-yair

first aid (n)
les premiers
secours (m)
*pruhm-yay
suh-koor*

fish (n)
un poisson
pwa-so(n)

fishing (n)
la pêche
pehsh

fishing boat (n)
un bateau de pêche
ba-toh duh pehsh

fit (adj)
en forme
ah(n) form

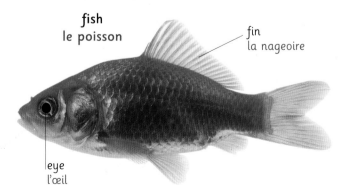

fish
le poisson

fin
la nageoire

eye
l'œil

a
b
c
d
e
Ff
g
h
i
j
k
l
m
n
o
p
q
r
s
t
u
v
w
x
y
z

flag
le drapeau

Ff

flag (n)
un drapeau
dra-poh

flashlight (n)
une lampe de poche
lahmp duh posh

flat (adj)
plat (m)
plate (f)
pla/plat

fleece (n)
une polaire
po-lair

flipper (n)
une palme
pahlm

flock (of sheep) (n)
un troupeau
troo-poh

flood (n)
une inondation
in-on-da-syo(n)

floor (n)
le sol
sol

flour (n)
la farine
fah-reen

flower (n)
une fleur
fluhr

flute (n)
une flûte
flewt

fly (n)
une mouche
moosh

fog (n)
le brouillard
broo-yar

food (n)
la nourriture
noo-ree-tewr

foot (human) (n)
un pied
pyay

foot (animal) (n)
une patte
pat

foreign (adj)
étranger (m)
ay-trahn-zhay

étrangère (f)
ay-trahn-zhair

forest (n)
une forêt
fo-reh

fork (n)
une fourchette
foor-shet

forward (adv)
en avant
ah(n) av-ah(n)

fox (n)
un renard
ruh-nar

frame (n)
un cadre
kah-druh

free time (n)
le temps libre
tah(n) lee-bruh

freedom (n)
la liberté
lee-bair-tay

freezer (n)
un congélateur
kon-zhey-la-tuhr

French (n)
le français
frahn-say

fresh (adj)
frais (m)
fraîche (f)
fray/frehsh

friend (n)
un ami une amie
a-mee

friendly (adj)
amical (m)
amicale (f)
a-mee-kal

fries (n)
des frites (f)
freet

frightened (adj)
effrayé (m)
effrayée (f)
eh-fray-yay

frog (n)
une grenouille
gruh-noo-ye

from (prep)
de
duh

front door (n)
une porte d'entrée
port dahn-tray

fruit (n)
un fruit
frwee

frying pan (n)
une poêle
pwal

fuel (n)
le carburant
kar-bew-rah(n)

full (adj)
plein (m)
pleine (f)
pla(n)/plen

fun (adj)
chouette
shoo-et

fur (n)
des poils (m)
pwal

furniture (n)
des meubles (m)
muh-bluh

future (n)
l'avenir (m)
lav-neer

frog
la grenouille

G

globe
le globe

game (n)
un jeu
zhuh

garage (n)
un garage
gar-azh

garbage (n)
des ordures (f)
or-dewr

garden (n)
un jardin
zhar-da(n)

gardener (n)
un jardinier
zhar-deen-yay

une jardinière
zhar-deen-yair

gardening (n)
le jardinage
zhar-dee-nazh

gas (n)
l'essence (f)
le-sahns

gas (as in stove) (n)
le gaz
gahz

gentle (adj)
doux (m) douce (f)
doo/dooss

gently (adv)
doucement
dooss-mah(n)

giant (n)
un géant
zhay-ah(n)

giraffe (n)
une girafe
zhee-raf

girl (n)
une fille
fee-ye

girlfriend (n)
une petite amie
puh-teet a-mee

glacier (n)
un glacier
glass-yay

glass (drink) (n)
un verre
vair

glasses (n)
des lunettes (f)
lew-net

globe (n)
un globe
glob

glove (n)
un gant
gah(n)

glue (n)
la colle
kol

goal (n)
un but
bewt

goat (n)
une chèvre
shay-vruh

God (n)
Dieu (m)
dyuh

goggles (n)
des lunettes de
natation (f)
*lew-net duh
na-ta-syo(n)*

gold (n)
l'or (m)
lor

goldfish (n)
un poisson rouge
pwa-so(n) roozh

golf (n)
le golf
golf

good (adj)
bon (m)
bonne (f)
bo(n)/bon

gorilla (n)
un gorille
go-ree-ye

government (n)
un gouvernement
goo-vairn-mah(n)

grandfather (n)
un grand-père
grahn pair

grandmother (n)
une grand-mère
grahn mair

grandparents (n)
des grands-parents (m)
grah(n) par-ah(n)

grape (n)
le raisin
ray-za(n)

grass (n)
l'herbe (f)
lairb

grasshopper (n)
une sauterelle
soht-rel

gray (adj)
gris (m) grise (f)
gree/greez

great (adj)
génial
zhay-nee-yal

green (adj)
vert (m) verte (f)
vair/vairt

greenhouse (n)
une serre
sair

ground (n)
la terre
tair

group (n)
un groupe
groop

guide (n)
un guide
gheed

guinea pig (n)
un cochon d'Inde
ko-sho(n) dand

guitar (n)
une guitare
ghee-tar

gymnastics (n)
la gymnastique
zheem-nas-teek

guitar
la guitare

a
b
c
d
e
f
Gg
h
i
j
k
l
m
n
o
p
q
r
s
t
u
v
w
x
y
z

a
b
c
d
e
f
g
Hh
i
j
k
l
m
n
o
p
q
r
s
t
u
v
w
x
y
z

70

hot-air balloon
la montgolfière

habitat (n)
un habitat
a-bee-ta

hair (animal) (n)
des poils (m)
pwal

hair (human) (n)
des cheveux (m)
shuh-vuh

hairbrush (n)
une brosse
à cheveux
bros ah shuh-vuh

hairdresser (n)
un coiffeur
kwa-fuhr

une coiffeuse
kwa-fuhz

hairy (adj)
poilu (m)
poilue (f)
pwa-lew

half (n)
une moitié
mwat-yay

hallway (n)
un couloir
kool-wahr

hamster (n)
un hamster
am-stair

hand (n)
une main
ma(n)

handbag (n)
un sac à main
sak ah ma(n)

handkerchief (n)
un mouchoir
moosh-wahr

hang glider (n)
un deltaplane
delta-plan

happy (adj)
content (m)
kon-tah(n)

contente (f)
kon-tahnt

harbor (n)
un port
por

hard (adj)
dur (m)
dure (f)
dewr

hard drive (n)
un disque dur
deesk dewr

hare (n)
un lièvre
lyeh-vruh

harvest (n)
une moisson
mwa-so(n)

hat (n)
un chapeau
sha-poh

hawk (n)
un faucon
foh-ko(n)

hay (n)
le foin
fwa(n)

he (pron)
il
eel

head (n)
une tête
teht

headache (n)
un mal de tête
mal duh teht

healthy (adj)
en bonne santé
ah(n) bon sahn-tay

heart (n)
un cœur
kuhr

heat (n)
la chaleur
sha-luhr

heavy (adj)
lourd (m)
lourde (f)
loor/loord

helicopter (n)
un hélicoptère
ay-lee-kop-tair

helmet (n)
un casque
kask

help (n)
une aide
ehd

her/his (adj)
son (m) sa (f)
so(n)/sa

her/him (pron)
la (her) le (him)
l' (before a vowel)
la/luh/l

hamster
le hamster

hero (n)
un héros
air-o

heron (n)
un héron
air-o(n)

hers/his (pron)
le sien (m)
luh sya(n)

la sienne (f)
la syen

hexagon (n)
un hexagone
exa-gone

hi
salut
sa-lew

hide-and-seek (n)
cache-cache (m)
kash kash

high (adj)
haut (m)
haute (f)
oh/oht

highway (n)
une autoroute
oh-toh-root

hill (n)
une colline
kol-leen

hip (n)
une hanche
ahnsh

historical (adj)
historique
ee-sto-reek

history (n)
l'histoire (f)
leest-wahr

hive (n)
une ruche
rewsh

hobby (n)
un loisir
lwa-zeer

hockey (n)
le hockey
oh-kay

hole (n)
un trou
troo

home (n)
la maison
may-zo(n)

homework (n)
des devoirs (m)
duhv-wahr

honey (n)
le miel
myel

hood (n)
une capuche
ka-pew-sh

horn (n)
une corne
korn

horrible (adj)
horrible
o-ree-bluh

horse (n)
un cheval
shuh-val

horseback riding (n)
l'équitation (f)
lay-kee-ta-syo(n)

hospital (n)
un hôpital
o-pee-tal

hot (adj)
chaud (m)
shoh

chaude (f)
shohd

hot-air balloon (n)
une montgolfière
mohn-golf-yair

hot chocolate (n)
un chocolat chaud
sho-ko-la shoh

hotdog (n)
un hot-dog
ot dog

hotel (n)
un hôtel
o-tel

hour (n)
l'heure (f)
luhr

house (n)
une maison
may-zo(n)

how (adv)
comment
ko-mah(n)

huge (adj)
énorme
ay-norm

human (n)
un être humain
eh-trew-ma(n)

hummingbird (n)
un oiseau-mouche
wa-zoh moosh

hungry (adj)
affamé (m)
affamée (f)
af-fa-may

honey
le miel

hurricane (n)
un ouragan
oo-ra-gah(n)

husband (n)
un mari
ma-ree

hut (n)
une cabane
ka-ban

Hh

a
b
c
d
e
f
g
Hh
i
j
k
l
m
n
o
p
q
r
s
t
u
v
w
x
y
z

horse
le cheval

a
b
c
d
e
f
g
h
Ii
j
k
l
m
n
o
p
q
r
s
t
u
v
w
x
y
z

island
l'île

I (pron)
je/j'
zhuh/zh

ice (n)
la glace
glass

ice cream (n)
une glace
glass

ice cube (n)
un glaçon
glass-o(n)

ice cream
la glace

ice hockey (n)
le hockey sur glace
oh-kay soor glass

ice pop (n)
un bâtonnet
ba-toh-nay

ice-skating (n)
le patinage sur glace
pa-tee-nazh soor glass

idea (n)
une idée
ee-day

ill (adj)
malade
ma-lad

illness (n)
une maladie
ma-la-dee

immediately (adv)
tout de suite
too duh sweet

important (adj)
important (m)
am-por-tah(n)

importante (f)
am-por-tahnt

impossible (adj)
impossible
am-po-see-bluh

information (n)
une information
an-for-ma-syo(n)

ingredient (n)
un ingrédient
an-gray-diah(n)

injury (n)
une blessure
bless-ewr

ink (n)
l'encre (f)
lahn-kruh

insect (n)
un insecte
an-sekt

inside (prep)
à l'intérieur de
ah lan-tayr-yuhr duh

instruction (n)
une instruction
an-strewk-syo(n)

instrument (n)
un instrument
an-strew-mah(n)

interesting (adj)
intéressant (m)
an-tair-ay-sah(n)

intéressante (f)
an-tair-ay-sahnt

international (adj)
international (m)
internationale (f)
an-tair-na-syo-nal

Internet (n)
l'Internet (m)
lin-tair-net

intersection (n)
un carrefour
kar-foor

into (prep)
dans
dah(n)

invitation (n)
une invitation
an-vee-ta-syo(n)

iron (clothes) (n)
un fer à repasser
fair ah ruh-pah-say

island (n)
une île
eel

its (adj)
son (m) sa (f)
so(n)/sa

it's (it is)
c'est
say

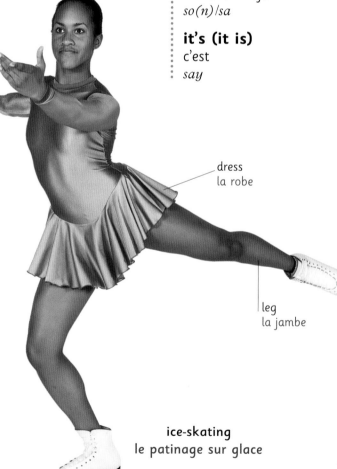

dress
la robe

leg
la jambe

ice-skating
le patinage sur glace

J

jug
la cruche

jacket (n)
un blouson
bloo-zo(n)

jam (n)
la confiture
kon-fee-tewr

jeans (n)
un jean
jeen

jellyfish (n)
une méduse
may-dewz

jet (n)
un avion à réaction
*av-yo(n) ah
ray-ak-syo(n)*

jewel (n)
un bijou
bee-zhoo

jewelry (n)
des bijoux (m)
bee-zhoo

job (n)
un emploi
am-plwa

joke (n)
une blague
blag

journey (n)
un voyage
vwa-yazh

judo (n)
le judo
zhew-doh

jug (n)
une cruche
krewsh

juice (n)
le jus
zhew

jump rope (n)
une corde à sauter
kord ah soh-tay

jungle (n)
la jungle
zhahn-gluh

just (adv)
juste
zhewst

jeans
le jean

K

kite
le cerf-volant

kangaroo (n)
un kangourou
kahn-goo-roo

karate (n)
le karaté
ka-ra-tay

kettle (n)
une bouilloire
booy-wahr

key (n)
une clé
klay

keyboard (n)
un clavier
klav-yay

kind (gentle) (adj)
gentil (m)
zhahn-tee

gentille (f)
zhahn-teeye

kind (type) (n)
une sorte
sort

king (n)
un roi
rwa

kiss (n)
un baiser
bay-zay

kitchen (n)
une cuisine
kwee-zeen

kite (n)
un cerf-volant
sair vo-lah(n)

kitten (n)
un chaton
sha-to(n)

knee (n)
un genou
zhuh-noo

knife (n)
un couteau
koo-toh

knight (n)
un chevalier
shuh-val-yay

knot (n)
un nœud
nuh

koala (n)
un koala
ko-a-la

kitten
le chaton

tail
la queue

a
b
c
d
e
f
g
h
i
Jj
Kk
l
m
n
o
p
q
r
s
t
u
v
w
x
y
z

73

L

a
b
c
d
e
f
g
h
i
j
k
Ll
m
n
o
p
q
r
s
t
u
v
w
x
y
z

lemon
le citron

ladder (n)
une échelle
ey-shell

ladybug (n)
une coccinelle
kok-see-nel

lake (n)
un lac
lak

lamb (n)
un agneau
an-yoh

lamp (n)
une lampe
lahmp

land (n)
un terrain
tair-ra(n)

language (n)
une langue
lahn-guh

laptop (n)
un ordinateur portable
or-dee-na-tuhr por-ta-bluh

last (adj)
dernier (m)
dairn-yay

dernière (f)
dairn-yair

late (adv)
en retard
ah(n) ruh-tar

law (n)
une loi
lwa

lawn (n)
une pelouse
puh-looz

lawn mower (n)
une tondeuse à gazon
ton-duhz ah gah-zo(n)

lazy (adj)
paresseux (m)
pa-re-suh

paresseuse (f)
pa-re-suhz

leaf (n)
une feuille
fuh-ye

leather (adj)
en cuir
ah(n) kweer

left (adj)
gauche
gohsh

left-handed (adj)
gaucher (m)
goh-shay

gauchère (f)
goh-shair

leg (n)
une jambe
zhahmb

lemon (n)
un citron
see-tro(n)

lemonade (n)
une limonade
lee-mon-ad

leopard (n)
un léopard
lay-o-par

lesson (n)
une leçon
le-so(n)

letter (n)
une lettre
let-truh

lettuce (n)
une laitue
lay-tew

level (adj)
plat (m) plate (f)
pla/plat

library (n)
une bibliothèque
bee-blee-yo-tek

lid (n)
un couvercle
koo-vair-kluh

life (n)
la vie
vee

lifeboat (n)
un bateau de sauvetage
ba-toh duh sohv-tazh

lifeguard (n)
un surveillant
de baignade
*soor-vay-ah(n)
duh bayn-yad*

life jacket (n)
un gilet de
sauvetage
*zhee-leh duh
so-vuh-tazh*

**light (not dark)
(adj)**
clair (m) claire (f)
klair

**light (not heavy)
(adj)**
léger (m)
légère (f)
lay-zhay/lay-zhehr

light (n)
une lumière
lewm-yair

lighthouse (n)
un phare
far

lightning (n)
un éclair
ay-klair

like (prep)
comme
kom

line (n)
une ligne
leen-ye

une queue
kuh

lion (n)
un lion
lee-yo(n)

liquid (n)
un liquide
lee-keed

list (n)
une liste
leest

little (adj)
petit (m) petite (f)
puh-tee/puh-teet

living room (n)
un salon
sal-o(n)

lizard
le lézard

M

lizard (n)
un lézard
lay-zar

long (adj)
long (m)
longue (f)
lo(n)/lon-guh

loose (adj)
large
larzh

(a) lot (adj)
beaucoup
boh-koo

loud (adj)
bruyant (m)
brew-yah(n)

bruyante (f)
brew-yahnt

lovely (adj)
adorable
a-do-ra-bluh

low (adj)
bas (m)
basse (f)
bah/bahss

lucky (adj)
chanceux (m)
shahn-suh

chanceuse (f)
shahn-suhz

luggage (n)
des bagages (m)
bag-azh

lunch (n)
le déjeuner
day-zhuh-nay

lunch box (n)
la boîte à déjeuner
bwat a deh-juh-neh

magnet
l'aimant

machine (n)
une machine
ma-sheen

magazine (n)
un magazine
ma-ga-zeen

magician (n)
un magicien (m)
ma-zhee-sya(n)

une magicienne (f)
ma-zhee-syen

magnet (n)
un aimant
eh-mah(n)

magnetic (adj)
magnétique
man-yet-eek

magnifying glass (n)
une loupe
loop

mail (n)
la poste
post

mailbox (n)
une boîte aux lettres
bwat oh let-truh

mail carrier (n)
un facteur
fak-tuhr

une factrice
fak-treess

main (adj)
principal (m)
principale (f)
prahn-see-pal

makeup (n)
le maquillage
ma-kee-yazh

male (human) (n)
un homme
om

mammal (n)
un mammifère
ma-mee-fair

man (n)
un homme
om

map (n)
une carte
kart

marbles (toy) (n)
des billes (f)
bee-ye

mark (grade) (n)
une note
noht

marker (n)
un feutre
fuh-truh

market (n)
un marché
mar-shay

married (adj)
marié (m) mariée (f)
mar-yay

mask (n)
un masque
mask

mat (n)
un petit tapis
puh-tee ta-pee

match (game) (n)
un match
match

matchbox (n)
une boîte d'allumettes
bwat dal-lew-met

math (n)
les mathématiques (f)
ma-tay-ma-teek

maybe (adv)
peut-être
puht-eh-truh

me (pron)
me/m' (vowel)
muh/m

meal (n)
un repas
ruh-pah

meaning (n)
un sens
sahnss

measurement (n)
une mesure
muh-zewr

meat (n)
la viande
vyahnd

medicine (n)
un médicament
may-dee-ka-mah(n)

melon (n)
un melon
muh-lo(n)

melon
le melon

a
b
c
d
e
f
g
h
i
j
k
Ll
Mm
n
o
p
q
r
s
t
u
v
w
x
y
z

75

a
b
c
d
e
f
g
h
i
j
k
l

Mm

n
o
p
q
r
s
t
u
v
w
x
y
z

milkshake
le milk-shake

menu (n)
la carte
kart

merry-go-round (n)
un tourniquet
toor-nee-kay

mess (n)
le désordre
day-zor-druh

message (n)
un message
mess-sazh

microwave (n)
un micro-ondes
mee-kro ond

middle (n)
le milieu
meel-yuh

midnight (n)
minuit (m)
mee-nwee

milk (n)
le lait
lay

milkshake (n)
un milk-shake
meelk shayk

million (n)
million
meel-yo(n)

mineral (n)
un minéral
mee-nay-ral

minute (n)
une minute
mee-newt

mirror (n)
un miroir
meer-wahr

mistake (n)
une erreur
er-ruhr

mitten (n)
une mitaine
mee-tehn

mixture (n)
un mélange
may-lahnzh

modeling clay (n)
la pâte à modeler
paht ah mod-lay

mom (n)
maman (f)
mah-mah(n)

money (n)
l'argent (m)
lar-zhah(n)

monkey (n)
un singe
sanzh

monster (n)
un monstre
mon-struh

mitten
la mitaine

month (n)
un mois
mwa

moon (n)
la lune
lewn

more than
plus que
plews kuh

morning (n)
le matin
ma-ta(n)

mosque (n)
une mosquée
mos-kay

moth (n)
un papillon de nuit
pa-pee-yo(n) duh nwee

mother (n)
une mère
mair

motor (n)
un moteur
mo-tuhr

motorcycle (n)
une moto
moh-toh

mountain (n)
une montagne
mon-tan-ye

mountain bike (n)
un V. T. T. (vélo tout
terrain)
vay-tay-tay

**mouse (animal)
(n)**
une souris
soo-ree

**mouse
(computer) (n)**
une souris
soo-ree

mouth (n)
une bouche
boosh

movie star (n)
une vedette de cinéma
vuh-det duh see-nay-ma

MP3 player (n)
un lecteur MP3
lek-tur em-peh-trwa

mud (n)
la boue
boo

muddy (adj)
boueux (m)
boo-uh

boueuse (f)
boo-uhz

mug (n)
une tasse
tahss

museum (n)
un musée
mew-zay

mushroom (n)
un champignon
shahm-pee-nio(n)

music (n)
la musique
mew-zeek

musician (n)
un musicien
mew-zee-sya(n)

une musicienne
mew-zee-syen

mustache (n)
une moustache
moose-tash

my (adj)
mon (m) ma (f)
mo(n)/ma

mushroom
le champignon

N

necklace
le collier

nail (n)
un ongle
ong-luh

name (n)
un nom
no(m)

narrow (adj)
étroit (m) étroite (f)
ay-trwa/ay-trwat

nature (n)
la nature
nat-ewr

naughty (adj)
vilain (m)
vee-la(n)

vilaine (f)
veelehn

nest
le nid

near (prep)
près de
preh duh

nearly (adv)
presque
presk

neck (n)
un cou
koo

necklace (n)
un collier
kol-yay

needle (n)
une aiguille
ehg-wee-ye

neighbor (n)
un voisin
vwa-za(n)

une voisine
vwa-zeen

nephew (n)
un neveu
nuh-vuh

nest (n)
un nid
nee

net (n)
une épuisette
ay-pwee-zet

never (adv)
jamais
zha-may

new (adj)
nouveau (m)
noo-voh

nouvelle (f)
noo-vel

news (n)
des nouvelles (f)
noo-vel

newspaper (n)
un journal
zhoor-nal

next (adj)
prochain (m)
pro-shah(n)

prochaine (f)
pro-shehn

nice (adj)
sympathique
sam-pa-teek

niece (n)
une nièce
nyehs

night (n)
la nuit
nwee

nobody (pron)
personne
pair-son

noisy (adj)
bruyant (m)
brew-yah(n)

bruyante (f)
brew-yahnt

noodles (n)
des nouilles (f)
noo-ye

north (n)
le nord
nor

nose (n)
un nez
nay

noodles
des nouilles

notebook (n)
un cahier
ka-yay

un carnet
kar-neh

nothing (n/pron)
rien (m)
rya(n)

now (adv)
maintenant
mehn-tuh-nah(n)

nowhere (adv)
nulle part
newl par

number (n)
un nombre
nom-bruh

nurse (n)
un infirmier (m)
an-feerm-yay

une infirmière (f)
an-feerm-yair

nursery (n)
une crèche
krehsh

marker
le feutre

notebook
le carnet

a
b
c
d
e
f
g
h
i
j
k
l
m

Nn

o
p
q
r
s
t
u
v
w
x
y
z

a
b
c
d
e
f
g
h
i
j
k
l
m
Oo
n
o
p
q
r
s
t
u
v
w
x
y
z

ocean
l'océan

oar (n)
une rame
rahm

object (n)
un objet
ob-zhay

ocean (n)
un océan
o-say-ah(n)

office (n)
un bureau
bew-roh

often (adv)
souvent
soo-vah(n)

oil (n)
l'huile (f)
lweel

old (adj)
vieux (m) vieille (f)
vyuh/vyay

old person (n)
une personne âgée
pair-son ah-zhay

Olympic Games (n)
des Jeux Olympiques (m)
zhuh-zo-lem-peek

on top of (prep)
sur
soor

onion (n)
un oignon
oh-nyo(n)

only (adv)
seulement
suhl-mah(n)

open (adj)
ouvert (m)
oo-vair

ouverte (f)
oo-vairt

opening hours (n)
des heures d'ouverture (f)
uhr doo-vair-tewr

operation (n)
une opération
o-pair-a-syo(n)

opposite (n)
un contraire
kon-trair

orange
l'orange

opposite (prep)
en face de
ah(n) fass duh

or (conj)
ou
oo

orange (color) (adj)
orange
o-ranzh

orange (fruit) (n)
une orange
o-ranzh

orange juice (n)
un jus d'orange
zhew do-ranzh

orchestra (n)
un orchestre
or-kes-truh

other (adj)
autre
oh-truh

ouch!
aïe !
eye-ye

our (adj)
notre
no-truh

orange juice
le jus d'orange

out of (prep)
hors de
or duh

outside (adv)
dehors
duh-or

oval (n)
un ovale
o-val

oven (n)
un four
foor

oven mitt (n)
un gant de cuisine
gah(n) duh kwee-zeen

over there (adv)
là-bas
la bah

owl (n)
un hibou
ee-boo

own (adj)
propre
pro-pruh

owl
le hibou

P

paint can
le pot de peinture

page (n)
une page
pazh

paint (n)
la peinture
pan-tewr

paint brush (n)
un pinceau
pan-soh

paint can (n)
un pot de peinture
poh duh pan-tewr

pair (n)
une paire
pair

pajamas (n)
un pyjama
pee-zha-ma

palm tree (n)
un palmier
palm-yay

pancake (n)
une crêpe
krehp

panda (n)
un panda
pahn-da

pants (n)
un pantalon
pahn-ta-lo(n)

paper (n)
le papier
pap-yay

paper clip (n)
un trombone
trom-bon

paper towel (n)
un essuie-tout
es-swee too

parade (n)
un défilé
day-fee-lay

parent (n)
un parent
par-ah(n)

park (n)
un parc
park

parrot (n)
un perroquet
pair-o-kay

part (of) (n)
une partie
par-tee

partner (n)
un/une camarade
ka-ma-rad

party (n)
une fête
feht

passenger (n)
un passager
pah-sa-zhay

une passagère
pah-sa-zhair

passport (n)
un passeport
pass-por

past (history) (n)
le passé
pah-say

past (prep)
après
ap-reh

pasta (n)
des pâtes (f)
paht

path (n)
un chemin
shuh-ma(n)

patient (adj)
patient (m)
pa-sya(n)

patiente (f)
pa-syant

patient (n)
un patient
pa-sya(n)

une patiente
pa-syant

pattern (n)
un motif
mo-teef

paw (n)
une patte
pat

pay (n)
un salaire
sa-lair

pea (n)
un petit pois
puh-tee pwa

pear
la poire

peace (n)
la paix
pay

peaceful (adj)
tranquille
trahn-keel

peanut (n)
une cacahuète
ka-ka-weht

pear (n)
une poire
pwahr

pebble (n)
un galet
ga-lay

pedal (n)
une pédale
pay-dal

pelican (n)
un pélican
peh-lee-ka(n)

wing
l'aile

beak
le bec

pelican
le pélican

a
b
c
d
e
f
g
h
i
j
k
l
m
n
o
Pp
q
r
s
t
u
v
w
x
y
z

79

a
b
c
d
e
f
g
h
i
j
k
l
m
n
o

Pp

q
r
s
t
u
v
w
x
y
z

pen (n)
un stylo
stee-loh

pencil (n)
un crayon à papier
kray-o(n) ah pap-yay

pencil case (n)
une trousse
trooss

penguin (n)
un manchot
mahn-shoh

pentagon (n)
un pentagone
pa(n)-ta-gone

people (n)
des gens (m) (pl)
zhah(n)

pepper (n)
le poivre
pwa-vruh

perfect (adj)
parfait (m)
par-fay

parfaite (f)
par-feht

perhaps (adv)
peut-être
puh-teh-truh

person (n)
une personne
pair-son

pet (n)
un animal de
compagnie
*ah-nee-mal duh
kom-pa-nee*

pharmacy (n)
une pharmacie
far-ma-see

phone (n)
un téléphone
tay-lay-fon

photo (n)
une photo
fo-toh

piano (n)
un piano
piano

piano
le piano

pinecone
la pomme de pin

picnic (n)
un pique-nique
peek neek

picture (n)
une image
ee-mazh

piece (n)
un morceau
mor-soh

pig (n)
un cochon
ko-sho(n)

pillow (n)
un oreiller
o-ray-yay

pilot (n)
un pilote
pee-lot

pineapple (n)
un ananas
ah-na-nass

pinecone (n)
une pomme de pin
pom duh pa(n)

pine tree (n)
un pin
pa(n)

ping-pong (n)
le tennis de table
ten-neess duh tab-luh

pink (adj)
rose
rohz

pizza (n)
une pizza
peed-za

place (n)
un endroit
ahn-drwa

plane (n)
un avion
av-yo(n)

planet (n)
une planète
plah-net

plant (n)
une plante
plahnt

plastic (adj)
en plastique
ah(n) plas-teek

plastic bag (n)
un sac en plastique
sak ah(n) plas-teek

pine tree
le pin

plate (n)
une assiette
a-see-yet

platform (n)
un quai
kay

play (theater) (n)
une pièce de théâtre
pyehs duh tay-a-truh

player (n)
un joueur
zhoo-uhr

une joueuse
zhoo-uhz

playground (n)
une cour de récréation
koor duh
ray-kray-a-syo(n)

playtime (n)
une récréation
ray-kray-a-syo(n)

please (adv)
s'il vous plaît (formal)
seel voo pleh

s'il te plaît (informal)
seel tuh pleh

plug (bath) (n)
une bonde
bond

plug (electric) (n)
une prise électrique
preez ay-lek-treek

pocket (n)
une poche
posh

pocket money (n)
l'argent de poche (m)
lar-zhah(n) duh posh

point (n)
un point
pwa(n)

polar bear (n)
un ours blanc
oorss blah(n)

pole (post) (n)
un poteau
po-toh

police (n)
la police
po-leess

police car (n)
une voiture de police
vwa-tewr duh po-leess

police helicopter (n)
un hélicoptère
de police
ay-lee-kop-tair
duh po-leess

pond (n)
un étang
ay-tah(n)

poor (adj)
pauvre
poh-vruh

popular (adj)
populaire
po-pew-lair

possible (adj)
possible
po-see-bluh

postcard (n)
une carte postale
kart pos-tal

poster (n)
une affiche
af-feesh

post office (n)
un bureau de poste
bew-roh duh post

potato (n)
une pomme
de terre
pom duh tair

puppy
le chiot

powder (n)
la poudre
poo-druh

present (n)
un cadeau
ka-doh

president (n)
un président
pray-zee-dah(n)

pretty (adj)
joli (m)
jolie (f)
zho-lee

price (n)
un prix
pree

prince (n)
un prince
pranss

princess (n)
une princesse
pran-sess

prize (n)
un prix
pree

probably (adv)
probablement
pro-bab-luh-mah(n)

problem (n)
un problème
prob-lehm

program (TV) (n)
une émission
ay-mee-syo(n)

project (n)
un projet
pro-zhay

pumpkin (n)
une citrouille
see-troo-ye

pupil (n)
un/une élève
ay-lehv

puppet (n)
une marionnette
mar-yon-net

puppet show (n)
un spectacle
de marionnettes
spek-tak-luh duh
mar-yon-net

puppy (n)
un chiot
shyoh

purple (adj)
violet (m)
violette (f)
vyo-lay/vyo-let

purse (n)
un porte-monnaie
port mo-nay

puzzle (n)
un puzzle
puh-zluh

a
b
c
d
e
f
g
h
i
j
k
l
m
n
o
Pp
q
r
s
t
u
v
w
x
y
z

81

a
b
c
d
e
f
g
h
i
j
k
l
m
n
o
p

Qq
Rr

s
t
u
v
w
x
y
z

Q R

queen
la reine

quarter (n)
un quart
kar

queen (n)
une reine
rehn

question (n)
une question
kest-yo(n)

quickly (adv)
vite
veet

quiet (adj)
silencieux (m)
see-lahn-syuh

silencieuse (f)
see-lahn-syuhz

quietly (adv)
tranquillement
trahn-keel-mah(n)

quiz (n)
un quiz
kweez

rabbit (n)
un lapin
la-pah(n)

race (n)
une course
koorss

race car (n)
une voiture de course
vwa-tewr duh koorss

racket (n)
une raquette
ra-ket

radio (n)
une radio
rad-yo

rain (n)
la pluie
plwee

rain forest (n)
la forêt tropicale
for-eh tro-pee-kal

rainbow (n)
un arc-en-ciel
ark en see-yel

raincoat (n)
un imperméable
am-pair-may-a-bluh

rake (n)
un râteau
rah-toh

raspberry (n)
une framboise
frahm-bwaz

rat (n)
un rat
ra

reading (n)
la lecture
lek-tewr

ready (adj)
prêt (m)
preh

prête (f)
preht

real (adj)
réel (m)
réelle (f)
ray-el

really (adv)
vraiment
vray-mah(n)

receipt (n)
un ticket de caisse
tee-kay duh kess

recipe (n)
une recette
ruh-set

rectangle (n)
un rectangle
rek-tahn-gluh

red (adj)
rouge
roozh

refrigerator (n)
un réfrigérateur
re-free-zhay-ra-tuhr

remote control (n)
une télécommande
tay-lay-kom-mahnd

report (school) (n)
un bulletin
bewl-tan(n)

rescue (n)
des secours (m)
suh-koor

restaurant (n)
un restaurant
res-tor-ah(n)

rhinoceros (n)
un rhinocéros
ree-no-say-ros

ribbon (n)
un ruban
rew-bah(n)

rice (n)
le riz
ree

rich (adj)
riche
reesh

right (not left) (adj)
droit (m) droite (f)
drwa/drwat

right (correct) (adj)
exact (m) exacte (f)
eg-zakt

ring (n)
une bague
bag

ripe (adj)
mûr (m)
mûre (f)
mewr

race car
la voiture de course

river (n)
une rivière
reev-yehr

road (n)
une route
root

robot (n)
un robot
ro-boh

rock (n)
un rocher
ro-shay

rocket (n)
une fusée
few-zay

rocket ship (n)
une fusée
few-zay

roll (bread) (n)
un petit pain
puh-tee pa(n)

rollerblade (n)
un roller
ro-lur

roof (n)
un toit
twa

room (n)
une pièce
pyehs

root (n)
une racine
ra-seen

rope (n)
une corde
kord

rose (n)
une rose
rohz

rough (adj)
rugueux (m)
rew-ghuh

rugueuse (f)
rew-ghuhz

round (adj)
rond (m)
ro(n)

ronde (f)
rond

route (n)
un trajet
tra-zhay

rowboat (n)
un canot
kanoh

rubber band (n)
un élastique
ay-la-steek

rug (n)
un tapis
ta-pee

rugby (n)
le rugby
rewg-bee

ruler (measure) (n)
une règle
reh-gluh

running (n)
la course à pied
koorss ah pyay

S

saddle
la selle

sack (n)
un sac
sak

sad (adj)
triste
treest

saddle (n)
une selle
sel

safe (adj)
en sécurité
ah(n) say-kew-ree-tay

sail (n)
une voile
vwal

sailboat (n)
un bateau à voiles
ba-toh ah vwal

sailor (n)
un marin
mar-a(n)

salad (n)
une salade
sal-ad

salesclerk (n)
un vendeur
vahn-duhr

une vendeuse
vahn-duhz

salt (n)
le sel
sel

same (adj)
même
mehm

sand (n)
le sable
sah-bluh

sandal (n)
une sandale
sahn-dahl

sandcastle (n)
un château de sable
sha-toh duh sah-bluh

sandwich (n)
un sandwich
sahnd-weetsh

saucepan (n)
une casserole
kass-rol

scarf (n)
une écharpe
eh-sharp

school (n)
l'école (f)
lay-kol

school bag (n)
un cartable
kar-ta-bluh

scarf
l'écharpe

a
b
c
d
e
f
g
h
i
j
k
l
m
n
o
p
q
Rr
Ss
t
u
v
w
x
y
z

83

a
b
c
d
e
f
g
h
i
j
k
l
m
n
o
p
q
r
Ss
t
u
v
w
x
y
z

scissors
des ciseaux

school uniform (n)
un uniforme scolaire
ew-nee-form sko-lair

science (n)
les sciences (f)
see-yahnss

scientist (n)
un/une scientifique
see-yahn-tee-feek

scissors (n)
des ciseaux
see-zoh

score (n)
un score
skor

screen (n)
un écran
ay-krah(n)

sea (n)
la mer
mair

seafood (n)
des fruits de mer
frwee duh mair

seagull (n)
une mouette
moo-wet

seal (n)
un phoque
fok

sea lion (n)
une otarie
oh-tah-ree

seaside (n)
le bord de mer
bor duh mair

season (n)
une saison
seh-zo(n)

seaweed (n)
une algue
al-guh

second (2nd) (adj)
deuxième
duhz-yehm

seed (n)
une graine
grehn

semicircle (n)
un demi-cercle
duh-mee sair-kluh

separately (adv)
séparément
say-pa-ray-mah(n)

shadow (n)
une ombre
om-bruh

shallow (adj)
peu profond (m)
puh pro-fo(n)

peu profonde (f)
puh pro-fond

shampoo (n)
un shampooing
shahm-pwa(n)

shape (n)
une forme
form

shark (n)
un requin
ruh-ka(n)

sharp (high-pitched) (adj)
aigu (m) aiguë (f)
ehg-ew

she (pron)
elle
el

sheep (n)
un mouton
moo-to(n)

sheepdog (n)
un chien de berger
shya(n) duh bair-zhay

sheet (for bed) (n)
un drap
dra

shelf (n)
une étagère
ay-ta-zhehr

shell (n)
un coquillage
ko-kee-yazh

shiny (adj)
brillant (m)
bree-yah(n)

brillante (f)
bree-yahnt

ship (n)
un navire
na-veer

shirt (n)
une chemise
shuh-meez

shoe (n)
une chaussure
shoh-soor

shop (n)
un magasin
ma-ga-za(n)

shopping (n)
des courses
koorss

shopping bag (n)
un sac
sak

shopping cart (n)
un caddie
ka-dee

shopping list (n)
une liste de courses
leest duh koorss

short (adj)
court (m) courte (f)
koor/koort

shorts (n)
un short
short

shoulder (n)
une épaule
eh-pohl

shovel (n)
une pelle
pel

show (n)
un spectacle
spek-ta-kluh

shower (n)
une douche
doosh

shy (adj)
timide
tee-meed

sick (adj)
malade
ma-lad

sidewalk (n)
un trottoir
trot-wahr

wool
la laine

sheep
le mouton

skateboard
le skate-board

sign (n)
un panneau
pan-noh

silver (n)
l'argent (m)
lar-zhah(n)

simple (adj)
simple
sam-pluh

singing (n)
le chant
shah(n)

sink (kitchen) (n)
un évier
eh-vyay

sink (bathroom) (n)
une lavabo
la-va-bo

sister (n)
une sœur
suhr

size (n)
la taille
tah-ye

skateboard (n)
un skate-board
skate board

skeleton (n)
un squelette
skuh-let

skiing (n)
le ski
skee

skin (n)
la peau
poh

skirt (n)
une jupe
zhewp

sky (n)
le ciel
syel

skyscraper (n)
un gratte-ciel
grat syel

sledge (n)
une luge
lewzh

sleeping bag (n)
un sac de
couchage
sak duh koosh-azh

sleeve (n)
une manche
mahn-sh

sleigh (n)
un traîneau
treh-noh

slipper (n)
une pantoufle
pahn-too-fluh

slow (adj)
lent (m)
lente (f)
lah(n)/lahnt

slowly (adv)
lentement
lahn-tuh-mah(n)

small (adj)
petit (m)
petite (f)
puh-tee/puh-teet

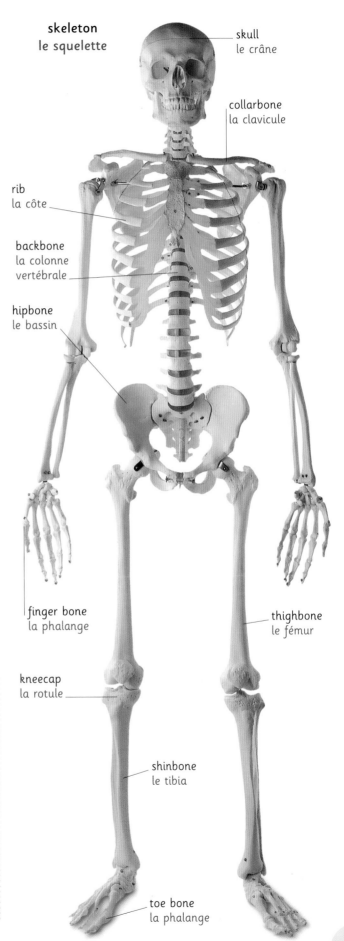

skeleton
le squelette

skull
le crâne

collarbone
la clavicule

rib
la côte

backbone
la colonne
vertébrale

hipbone
le bassin

finger bone
la phalange

thighbone
le fémur

kneecap
la rotule

shinbone
le tibia

toe bone
la phalange

a
b
c
d
e
f
g
h
i
j
k
l
m
n
o
p
q
r

Ss

t
u
v
w
x
y
z

tail
la queue

snake
le serpent

head
la tête

smartphone (n)
un smartphone
smart-fon

smell (n)
une odeur
o-duhr

smoke (n)
la fumée
few-may

smooth (adj)
lisse
leess

snail (n)
un escargot
es-kar-goh

snake (n)
un serpent
sair-pah(n)

sneakers (n)
des baskets (f)
bas-ket

snow (n)
la neige
nehzh

snowball (n)
une boule de neige
bool duh nehzh

snowboard (n)
un snow-board
snow board

snowflake (n)
un flocon de neige
flo-ko(n) duh nehzh

snowman (n)
un bonhomme de neige
bon-om duh nehzh

soap (n)
le savon
sa-vo(n)

soccer ball (n)
un ballon de football
ba-lo(n) duh foot-bohl

soccer game (n)
le football
foot-bohl

sock (n)
une chaussette
shoh-set

sofa (n)
un canapé
ka-na-pay

soft (adj)
doux (m) douce (f)
doo/dooss

soil (n)
la terre
tair

soldier (n)
un soldat
sol-da

solid (n)
un solide
sol-eed

some (adj)
quelques
kel-kuh

someone (pron)
quelqu'un
kel-ka(n)

something (pron)
quelque chose
kel-kuh shohz

sometimes (adv)
quelquefois
kel-kuh fwa

soon (adv)
bientôt
byan-toh

south (n)
le sud
sood

souvenir (n)
un souvenir
soov-neer

space (n)
l'espace (m)
less-pass

spaghetti (n)
des spaghettis (m)
spa-geh-tee

Spanish (n)
l'espagnol (m)
le-span-yol

speakers (n)
des hauts-parleurs (m)
oh par-lur

special (adj)
particulier (m)
par-tee-kewl-yay

particulière (f)
par-tee-kewl-yair

speech (n)
un discours
dee-skoor

sphere (n)
une sphère
sfair

spider (n)
une araignée
ah-reh-nyay

sponge (n)
une éponge
ay-ponzh

spoon (n)
une cuillère
kwee-yehr

sport (n)
un sport
spor

spots (n)
des taches (f)
tash

spring (season) (n)
le printemps
pran-tah(m)

square (n)
un carré
kar-ray

squirrel (n)
un écureuil
ay-kew-ruh-ye

snail
l'escargot

86

starfish
l'étoile de mer

stairs (n)
un escalier
es-kal-yay

stamp (n)
un timbre
tam-bruh

star (n)
une étoile
ay-twal

starfish (n)
une étoile de mer
ay-twal duh mair

station (n)
une gare
gar

steam (n)
la buée
bway

steep (adj)
raide
rehd

stem (n)
une tige
teezh

step (n)
un pas
pa

stepbrother (n)
un demi-frère
duh-mi frair

stepfather (n)
un beau-père
boh pair

stepmother (n)
une belle-mère
bel mair

stepsister (n)
une demi-sœur
duh-mi suhr

stick (n)
un bâton
bah-to(n)

sticker (n)
un autocollant
oh-to-ko-lah(n)

sticky (adj)
collant (m)
ko-lah(n)

collante (f)
ko-lahnt

stiff (adj)
raide
rehd

still (adj)
immobile
im-mo-beel

stomach (n)
un estomac
es-to-ma

stone (n)
une pierre
pyair

stormy (adj)
orageux (m)
or-azh-uh

orageuse (f)
or-azh-uhz

story (building) (n)
un étage
ay-tazh

story (n)
une histoire
eest-wahr

stove (n)
une cuisinière
kwee-zeen-yair

straight (adj)
droit (m)
droite (f)
drwa/drwat

strange (adj)
étrange
ay-trahnzh

straw (n)
la paille
pah-ye

strawberry (n)
une fraise
frehz

street (n)
une rue
rew

strawberry
la fraise

streetlight (n)
un réverbère
ray-vair-bair

strict (adj)
sévère
say-vehr

string (n)
une ficelle
fee-sel

stripes (n)
des rayures (f)
rey-yewr

stroller (n)
une poussette
poo-set

strong (adj)
fort (m)
forte (f)
for/fort

stupid (adj)
stupide
stoo-peed

stylish (adj)
élégant (m)
ay-lay-gah(n)

élégante (f)
ay-lay-gahnt

subject (n)
un sujet
soo-zhay

submarine (n)
un sous-marin
soo ma-ra(n)

subway (n)
un métro
may-troh

suddenly (adv)
tout à coup
toot ah koo

sugar (n)
le sucre
soo-kruh

suit (n)
un costume
kos-tewm

a
b
c
d
e
f
g
h
i
j
k
l
m
n
o
p
q
r
Ss
t
u
v
w
x
y
z

a
b
c
d
e
f
g
h
i
j
k
l
m
n
o
p
q
r

Ss
Tt

u
v
w
x
y
z

suitcase (n)
une valise
va-leez

summer (n)
l'été (m)
lay-tay

sun (n)
le soleil
so-laye

sun hat (n)
un chapeau
sha-poh

sunblock (n)
la crème solaire
krem soh-lair

sunflower (n)
un tournesol
toor-nuh-sol

sunglasses (n)
des lunettes de soleil (f)
lew-net duh so-laye

sunny (adj)
ensoleillé (m)
ensoleillée (f)
ahn-so-lay-yay

sunset (n)
un coucher de soleil
koo-shay duh so-laye

supermarket (n)
un supermarché
soo-pair-mar-shay

sure (adj)
sûr (m)
sûre (f)
soor

surface (n)
une surface
soor-fass

surfboard (n)
une planchede surf
plahnsh duh surf

surfing (n)
le surf
surf

surprise (n)
une surprise
soor-preez

surprising (adj)
étonnant (m)
ay-ton-nah(n)

étonnante (f)
ay-ton-nahnt

swan (n)
un cygne
seen-ye

sweater (n)
un pull
pewl

swimming (n)
la natation
na-ta-syo(n)

swimming pool (n)
une piscine
pee-seen

swimsuit (n)
un maillot de bain
ma-yoh duh ba(n)

swing (n)
une balançoire
ba-lahn-swahr

sunglasses
des lunettes de soleil

tadpole
le têtard

table (n)
une table
tab-luh

tadpole (n)
un têtard
teh-tar

tail (n)
une queue
kuh

tall (adj)
grand (m)
grah(n)

grande (f)
grahnd

tape measure (n)
un mètre
meh-truh

taxi (n)
un taxi
tak-see

tea (n)
le thé
tay

T

teacher (elementary school) (n)
un maître
meh-truh

une maîtresse
meh-tress

team (n)
une équipe
ay-keep

teddy bear (n)
un ours en peluche
oorss ah(n) puh-lewsh

telescope (n)
un télescope
tay-leh-skop

television (n)
une télévision
tay-lay-vee-zyo(n)

tennis (n)
le tennis
ten-neess

tent (n)
une tente
tahnt

term (n)
un mot
moh

terrible (adj)
terrible
teh-ree-bluh

text message (n)
un texto
teks-toh

that one (pron)
celui-là
suhl-wee-la

tape measure
le mètre

tongue
la langue

toad
le crapaud

the (article)
le (m) la (f) l'
(before a vowel)
luh/la/l

their (adj)
leur
luhr

then (conj)
alors
ah-lor

there (adv)
là
la

thermometer (n)
un thermomètre
tair-mo-meh-truh

they (pron)
ils (m) elles (f)
eel/el

thick (adj)
épais (m) épaisse (f)
eh-pay/eh-pehss

thin (adj)
fin (m) fine (f)
fa(n)/feen

thing (n)
une chose
shohz

third (adj)
troisième
trwaz-yehm

thirsty (adj)
assoiffé (m)
assoiffée (f)
a-swa-fay

this one (pron)
celui-ci
suhl-wee see

thousand (n)
mille
meel

through (prep)
à travers
ah tra-vair

thumb (n)
un pouce
pooss

thumbtack (n)
une punaise
pew-nehz

thunderstorm (n)
un orage
or-azh

ticket (n)
un billet
bee-yay

tide (n)
la marée
ma-ray

tie (n)
une cravate
kra-vat

tiger (n)
un tigre
tee-gruh

tight (adj)
serré (m) serrée (f)
sair-ray

tights (n)
des collants (m)
ko-lah(n)

time (n)
l'heure (f)
luhr

timetable (n)
un horaire
or-air

tiny (adj)
minuscule
mee-new-skewl

tired (adj)
fatigué (m)
fatiguée (f)
fa-tee-gay

tissues (n)
des mouchoirs
en papier (m)
*moosh-wahrs
ah(n) pap-yay*

toad (n)
un crapaud
kra-poh

toaster (n)
un grille-pain
gree-ye pa(n)

today (adv)
aujourd'hui
oh-zhoor-dwee

toe (n)
un orteil
or-teye

together (adv)
ensemble
ahn-sahm-bluh

toilet (n)
les toilettes
twa-let

toilet paper (n)
le papier toilette
pap-yay twa-let

tomato (n)
une tomate
tom-at

**tomorrow
(adv)**
demain
duh-ma(n)

tongue (n)
une langue
lahng

whiskers
des
moustaches

tiger
le tigre

stripes
des rayures

tail
la queue

a
b
c
d
e
f
g
h
i
j
k
l
m
n
o
p
q
r
s
Tt
u
v
w
x
y
z

89

a
b
c
d
e
f
g
h
i
j
k
l
m
n
o
p
q
r
s

Tt

u
v
w
x
y
z

toothbrush
la brosse
à dents

tonight (adv)
cette nuit
set nwee

too (adv)
aussi
oh-see

tool (n)
un outil
oo-tee

tooth (n)
une dent
dah(n)

toothbrush (n)
une brosse à dents
bros ah dah(n)

toothpaste (n)
le dentifrice
dahn-tee-freess

top (n)
le haut
oh

tornado (n)
une tornade
tor-nad

tortoise (n)
une tortue
tor-tew

toucan (n)
un toucan
too-kah(n)

tortoise
la tortue

tough (adj)
dur (m) dure (f)
dewr

tourist (n)
un/une touriste
too-reest

toward (prep)
vers
vair

towel (n)
une serviette
sair-vee-et

town (n)
une ville
veel

toy (n)
un jouet
zhoo-way

toy blocks (n)
des cubes (m)
kewb

toy box (n)
un coffre à jouets
koh-fra-joo-wey

tractor (n)
un tracteur
trak-tuhr

traffic (n)
la circulation
seer-kew-lah-syo(n)

traffic cone (n)
un cône de
signalisation
*uhn kohn duh
seen-nya-lee-za-syo(n)*

traffic lights (n)
des feux de
signalisation (m)
*fuh duh
seen-nya-lee-za-syo(n)*

train (n)
un train
tra(n)

train set (toy) (n)
un train
tra(n)

traffic lights
des feux de signalisation

train station (n)
une gare
gar

transportation (n)
le transport
trahn-spor

trash can (n)
une poubelle
poo-bell

tray (n)
un plateau
pla-toh

tree (n)
un arbre
ar-bruh

triangle (n)
un triangle
tree-yahn-gluh

trip (n)
un voyage
vwa-yazh

tropical (adj)
tropical (m)
tropicale (f)
tro-pee-kal

trouble (n)
un ennui
ahn-wee

trowel (n)
un déplantoir
day-plahnt-wahr

truck (n)
un camion
kam-yo(n)

true (adj)
vrai (m) vraie (f)
vray

trunk (animal) (n)
une trompe
tromp

trunk (tree) (n)
un tronc
tro(n)

trunks (swimming) (n)
un maillot de bain
ma-yoh duh ba(n)

T-shirt (n)
un tee-shirt
tee-shirt

tube (n)
un tube
tewb

tummy (n)
un ventre
vahn-truh

tunnel (n)
un tunnel
tew-nel

tractor
le tracteur

turkey
le dindon

U

uniform
l'uniforme

V

turkey (n)
un dindon
dan-do(n)

turn (bend) (n)
un tournant
toor-nah(n)

turtle (n)
une tortue de mer
tor-tew duh mair

twice (adv)
deux fois
duh fwa

twin (n)
un jumeau
zhew-moh

une jumelle
zhew-mel

tire (n)
un pneu
puh-nuh

ugly (adj)
laid (m) laide (f)
lay/lehd

umbrella (rain) (n)
un parapluie
pa-ra-plwee

umbrella (sun) (n)
un parasol
pa-ra-sol

uncle (n)
un oncle
onk-luh

under (prep)
sous
soo

underwear (n)
des sous-vêtements (m)
soo veht-mah(n)

unfair (adj)
injuste
an-zhewst

uniform (n)
un uniforme
ew-nee-form

universe (n)
un univers
ew-nee-vair

until (prep)
jusqu'à
zhew-ska

unusual (adj)
inhabituel (m)
inhabituelle (f)
ee-nah-bee-tew-el

upside down (adv)
à l'envers
ah lahn-vair

upstairs (adv)
en haut
ah(n) oh

useful (adj)
utile
ew-teel

usually (adv)
d'habitude
da-bee-tewd

vacation (n)
des vacances (f)
vak-ahnss

van (n)
une camionnette
kam-yon-net

vegetable (n)
un légume
lay-gewm

vegetarian (n)
un végétarien
vay-zhay-ta-rya(n)

une végétarienne
vay-zhay-ta-ryen

verb (n)
un verbe
vairb

very (adv)
très
treh

vet (n)
un/une vétérinaire
vay-tair-ee-nair

video game (n)
un jeu vidéo
zhuh vee-day-oh

village (n)
un village
vee-lazh

violin (n)
un violon
vyo-lo(n)

umbrella
le parapluie

violin
le violon

a
b
c
d
e
f
g
h
i
j
k
l
m
n
o
p
q
r
s
Tt
Uu
Vv
w
x
y
z

91

W

a
b
c
d
e
f
g
h
i
j
k
l
m
n
o
p
q
r
s
t
u
v

Ww

x
y
z

waist (n)
la taille
tah-ye

waiter (n)
un garçon de café
gar-so(n) duh ka-fay

waitress (n)
une serveuse
sair-vuhz

walk (n)
une promenade
pro-muh-nad

wall (n)
un mur
mewr

war (n)
une guerre
gair

wardrobe (n)
une armoire
arm-wahr

warm (adj)
chaud (m)
chaude (f)
shoh/shohd

warning (n)
un avertissement
ah-vair-tee-smah(n)

washcloth (n)
une serviette
de toilette
sair-vee-et duh twa-let

**washing
machine (n)**
une machine à laver
ma-sheen ah la-vay

watering can
l'arrosoir

wasp (n)
une guêpe
gehp

watch (n)
une montre
mon-truh

water (n)
l'eau (f)
loh

water lily (n)
un nénuphar
nay-new-far

watering can (n)
un arrosoir
ah-ro-zwar

watermelon (n)
une pastèque
pas-tehk

waterslide (n)
le toboggan aquatique
to-bo-ga(n) a-kwa-tik

wave (n)
une vague
vahg

we (pron)
nous
noo

weak (adj)
faible
fay-bluh

weather (n)
le temps
tah(n)

website (n)
un site web
seet web

weed (n)
une mauvaise herbe
moh-vayz airb

week (n)
une semaine
suh-mehn

weekend (n)
un week-end
week end

welcome (adj)
bienvenu (m)
bienvenue (f)
byan-vuh-new

well (adj)
bien
bya(n)

west (n)
l'ouest (m)
lwest

wet (adj)
mouillé (m)
mouillée (f)
moo-yay

whale (n)
une baleine
ba-len

wheat (n)
le blé
blay

wheel (n)
une roue
roo

wheelbarrow (n)
une brouette
broo-et

wheelchair (n)
un fauteuil roulant
foh-tuh-ye roo-lah(n)

when (adv)
quand
kah(n)

where (adv)
où
oo

while (conj)
pendant que
pahn-dah(n) kuh

whisker (n)
une moustache
moose-tash

whistle (n)
un sifflement
see-fluh-mah(n)

white (adj)
blanc (m)
blanche (f)
blah(n)/blahnsh

who (pron)
qui
kee

why (adv)
pourquoi
poor-kwa

wide (adj)
large
larzh

wife (n)
une épouse
ay-pooz

wave
la vague

wing
l'aile

wind (n)
le vent
vah(n)

window (n)
une fenêtre
fuh-neh-truh

windy (adj)
il y a du vent
eel ya dew vah(n)

wing (n)
une aile
ehl

winner (n)
un gagnant
gan-yah(n)

une gagnante
gan-yahnt

winter (n)
l'hiver (m)
lee-vair

with (prep)
avec
av-ek

without (prep)
sans
sah(n)

wolf (n)
un loup
loo

woman (n)
une femme
fam

wood (n)
le bois
bwa

wooden (adj)
en bois
ah(n) bwa

wool (n)
la laine
lehn

wool hat (n)
un bonnet
bon-nay

word (n)
un mot
moh

world (n)
un monde
mond

worm (n)
un ver
vair

worst (adj)
pire
peer

writing (act of) (n)
l'écriture (f)
lay-kree-tewr

Y

yacht
le yacht

yacht (n)
un yacht
yoht

year (n)
un an (for numbers)
une année
ah(n)/an-nay

yellow (adj)
jaune
zhohn

yesterday (adv)
hier
yair

yogurt (n)
un yaourt
ya-oort

you (pron)
tu (sing) vous (plu)
tew/voo

young (adj)
jeune
zhuhn

your (adj)
ton/ta (sing) votre (plu)
to(n)/ta
vo-truh

Z

zebra
le zèbre

zebra (n)
un zèbre
zeh-bruh

zip code (n)
un code postal
kohd pos-tal

zipper (n)
une fermeture éclair
fair-muh-ture ay-klair

zone (n)
une zone
zohn

zoo (n)
un zoo
zoh

zipper
la fermeture éclair

a
b
c
d
e
f
g
h
i
j
k
l
m
n
o
p
q
r
s
t
u
v
Ww
x
Yy
Zz

Aa

b
c
d
e
f
g
h
i
j
k
l
m
n
o
p
q
r
s
t
u
v
w
x
y
z

French A–Z

In this section, French words are in alphabetical order. Each one is followed by its English translation and a few letters to show what type of word it is—for example, a noun (n) or an adjective (adj).

Nouns in French are either masculine (m) or feminine (f). Sometimes a word in French might mean more than one thing in English, so there might be two translations underneath. Most of the nouns (naming words) here describe just one thing so they are singular.

To make a noun plural (more than one thing) you usually just add an "s"—the same as in English—though you do not pronounce it. In French, other words in the sentence change too—*le* and *la* become *les*, and *un* and *une* become *des*.

The adjectives also change, usually getting an extra "s" at the end.

> **(n)** = noun (a naming word). Either masculine or feminine. Feminine nouns usually have an "e" at the end.
> **(adj)** = adjective (a describing word). These words can change depending whether the noun they are describing is masculine (m) or feminine (f).
> **(adv)** = adverb (a word that gives more information about a verb, an adjective, or another adverb)
> **(conj)** = conjunction (a joining word; for example, "and")
> **(prep)** = preposition (for example, "about")
> **(pron)** = pronoun (for example, "he," "she," "it")
> **(article)** = (for example, "a," "an," "the")
> **(sing)** = singular (one thing) **(plu)** = plural (lots of things)
> **(m)** = masculine **(f)** = feminine

à l'arrière (adv)
back (opposite of front)

à l'envers (adv)
upside down

à l'intérieur de (prep)
inside

à la mode (adv)
fashionable

à travers (prep)
through

abeille (n) (f)
bee

absent/absente (adj)
away

accident (n) (m)
accident

activité (n) (f)
activity

addition (n) (f)
bill, check

adorable (adj)
lovely

adresse (n) (f)
address

adresse électronique (n) (f)
email address

adulte (n) (m/f)
adult

aéroport (n) (m)
airport

affaires (n) (f)
business

affamé/affamée (adj)
hungry

affiche (n) (f)
poster

âge (n) (m)
age

agneau (n) (m)
lamb

aide (n) (f)
help

aïe !
ouch!

aigle (n) (m)
eagle

aigu/aiguë (adj)
sharp (sound)

aiguille (n) (f)
needle

aile (n) (f)
wing

aimant (n) (m)
magnet

air (n) (m)
air

algue (n) (f)
seaweed

alligator (n) (m)
alligator

alors (conj)
then

alphabet (n) (m)
alphabet

ambulance (n) (f)
ambulance

ami/amie (n) (m/f)
friend

amical/amicale (adj)
friendly

ampoule (n) (f)
bulb (light)

amusement (n) (m)
fun

ananas (n) (m)
pineapple

ancre (n) (f)
anchor

anglais (n) (m)
English

animal (n) (m)
animal

animal de compagnie (n) (m)
pet

année/an (n) (f/m)
year

anniversaire (n) (m)
birthday

antenne (n) (f)
antenna

appareil photo (n) (m)
camera

apparence (n) (f)
appearance

appartement (n) (m)
apartment

appli (n) (f)
app

après (prep)
after, past

après-midi (n) (m)
afternoon

araignée (n) (f)
spider

arbre (n) (m)
tree

arc-en-ciel (n) (m)
rainbow

arche (n) (f)
arch

argent (n) (m)
money, silver

argent de poche (n) (m)
pocket money

armée (n) (f)
army

armoire (n) (f)
wardrobe

arrêt de bus (n) (m)
bus stop

arrivée (n) (f)
arrival

arrosoir (n) (m)
watering can

art (n) (m)
art

artiste (n) (m/f)
artist

ascenseur (n) (m)
elevator

assez (adv)
enough

assiette (n) (f)
plate

assistant/assistante (n) (m/f)
assistant

assoiffé/assoiffée (adj)
thirsty

astronaute (n) (m/f)
astronaut

astronome (n) (m/f)
astronomer

athlétisme (n) (m)
athletics

atlas (n) (m)
atlas

au-dessous de (prep)
below

au-dessus de (prep)
above

aujourd'hui (adv)
today

au rez-de-chaussée (adv)
downstairs

aussi (adv)
also, too

autobus (n) (m)
(public) bus

autocar (n) (m)
bus

autocollant (n) (m)
sticker

automne (n) (m)
fall, autumn

autoroute (n) (f)
highway

autour (prep)
around

autre (adj)
other

avant (prep)
before

avec (prep)
with

avenir (n) (m)
future

aventure (n) (f)
adventure

avertissement (n) (m)
warning

avion (n) (m)
airplane

avion à réaction (n) (m)
jet

avocat (n) (m)
avocado

B

babouin (n) (m)
baboon

badge (n) (m)
badge

badminton (n) (m)
badminton

bagages (n) (m)
luggage

bague (n) (f)
ring

baignoire (n) (f)
bath

baiser (n) (m)
kiss

balai (n) (m)
broom

balançoire (n) (f)
swing

balcon (n) (m)
balcony

baleine (n) (f)
whale

balle (n) (f)
ball

ballon (n) (m)
ball, balloon

ballon de football (n) (m)
soccer ball

banane (n) (f)
banana

banc (n) (m)
bench

bande-dessinée (n) (f)
comic (book)

banque (n) (f)
bank (money)

barbe (n) (f)
beard

barbecue (n) (m)
barbecue

barrière (n) (f)
fence

bas/basse (adj)
low

base-ball (n) (m)
baseball

basket-ball (n) (m)
basketball

baskets (n) (f)
sneakers

bataille (n) (f)
battle

bateau (n) (m)
boat

bateau à voile (n) (m)
sailboat

bateau de pêche (n) (m)
fishing boat

bateau de sauvetage (n) (m)
lifeboat

bâtiment (n) (m)
building

bâton (n) (m)
stick

Bb
Cc

a

bâtonnet de glace (n) (m)
ice pop

batte (n) (f)
bat (sports)

d

batterie (n) (f)
drum kit

e

beau/belle (adj)
beautiful

f

beaucoup (adv)
(a) lot

g

beau-père (n) (m)
stepfather

h

beauté (n) (f)
beauty

i

bébé (n) (m)
baby

j

bec (n) (m)
beak

k

belle-mère (n) (f)
stepmother

l

bête (n) (f)
creature

m

beurre (n) (m)
butter

n

bibliothèque (n) (f)
library

o

bien (adj)
fine

p

bien (adv)
well

q

bientôt (adv)
soon

r

bienvenu/bienvenue (adj)
welcome

s

t

bijou (n) (m)
jewel

u

bijoux (n) (m)
jewelry

v

billes (n) (f)
marbles (toy)

w

x

billet (n) (m)
bill (paper money), ticket

y

z

biscuit (n) (m)
cookie

blague (n) (f)
joke

blanc/blanche (adj)
white

blé (n) (m)
wheat

blessure (n) (f)
injury

bleu/bleue (adj)
blue

blond/blonde (adj)
blonde

blouson (n) (m)
jacket

bois (n) (m)
wood

boisson (n) (f)
drink

boîte (n) (f)
box

boîte à déjeuner (n) (f)
lunch box

boîte aux lettres (n) (f)
mailbox

boîte d'allumettes (n) (f)
matchbox

bol (n) (m)
bowl (cereal)

bon/bonne (adj)
good

bonbon (n) (m)
candy

bonde (n) (f)
plug

bondé/bondée (adj)
crowded

bonhomme de neige (n) (m)
snowman

bon marché (adj)
cheap

bonnet (n) (m)
wool hat

bord (n) (m)
edge

bord de la mer (n) (m)
seaside

botte (n) (f)
boot

bouche (n) (f)
mouth

boucle d'oreille (n) (f)
earring

boue (n) (f)
mud

bouée (n) (f)
buoy

boueux/boueuse (adj)
muddy

bougie (n) (f)
candle

bouilloire (n) (f)
kettle

boulangerie (n) (f)
bakery

boule de neige (n) (f)
snowball

boussole (n) (f)
compass

bouteille (n) (f)
bottle

bouton (n) (m)
button

bracelet (n) (m)
bracelet

branche (n) (f)
branch

bras (n) (m)
arm

brillant/brillante (adj)
bright, shiny

brise (n) (f)
breeze

brosse à cheveux (n) (f)
hairbrush

brosse à dents (n) (f)
toothbrush

brouette (n) (f)
wheelbarrow

brouillard (n) (m)
fog

bruyant/bruyante (adj)
loud, noisy

buée (n) (f)
steam

buisson (n) (m)
bush

bulbe (n) (m)
bulb (plant)

bulle (n) (f)
bubble

bulletin (n) (m)
report (for school)

bureau (n) (m)
desk, office

bureau de poste (n) (m)
post office

but (n) (m)
goal

c'est
it's (it is)

cabane (n) (f)
hut

cabinet médical (n) (m)
doctor's office

cacahuète (n) (f)
peanut

cache-cache (n) (m)
hide-and-seek

caddie (n) (m)
shopping cart

cadeau (n) (m)
present

cadre (n) (m)
frame

café (n) (m)
café, coffee

cage (n) (f)
cage

cahier (n) (m)
notebook

caisse (n) (f)
checkout, cash register

calculatrice (n) (f)
calculator

calendrier (n) (m)
calendar

calme (adj)
calm

camarade (n) (m/f)
partner

camion (n) (m)
truck

camion de pompier (n) (m)
fire truck

camionnette (n) (f)
van

campagne (n) (f)
countryside

canapé (n) (m)
sofa

canard (n) (m)
duck

caneton (n) (m)
duckling

cannette (n) (f)
can (drink)

canoë (n) (m)
canoe

canot (n) (m)
rowboat

cape (n) (f)
cloak

capitale (n) (f)
capital

capuche (n) (f)
hood

carburant (n) (m)
fuel

carnet (n) (m)
notebook

carotte (n) (f)
carrot

carré (n) (m)
square

carrefour (n) (m)
intersection

cartable (n) (m)
school bag

carte (n) (f)
card, map, menu

carte d'anniversaire (n) (f)
birthday card

carte postale (n) (f)
postcard

cartes (n) (f)
cards (playing)

carton (n) (m)
cardboard

casque (n) (m)
helmet

casquette (n) (f)
cap

cassé/cassée (adj)
broken

casserole (n) (f)
saucepan

cave (n) (f)
cellar

CD (n) (m)
CD

ceinture (n) (f)
belt

célèbre (adj)
famous

celui-ci (pron)
this one

celui-là (pron)
that one

centre (n) (m)
center

cercle (n) (m)
circle

céréale (n) (f)
cereal

cerf (n) (m)
deer

cerf-volant (n) (m)
kite

certain/certaine (adj)
certain

cerveau (n) (m)
brain

cette nuit
tonight

chaîne (n) (f)
chain

chaise (n) (f)
chair

chaise longue (n) (f)
deck chair

chaleur (n) (f)
heat

chambre (n) (f)
bedroom

chameau (n) (m)
camel

champ (n) (m)
field

champignon (n) (m)
mushroom

chanceux/chanceuse (adj)
lucky

changement (n) (m)
change

chant (n) (m)
singing

chapeau (n) (m)
hat, sun hat

chaque (adj)
each

charrette (n) (f)
cart

chat (n) (m)
cat

château de sable (n) (m)
sandcastle

chaton (n) (m)
kitten

chaud/chaude (adj)
hot, warm

chaussette (n) (f)
sock

chaussure (n) (f)
shoe

chauve-souris (n) (f)
bat (animal)

chef (n) (m/f)
chef/boss

chemin (n) (m)
path

cheminée (n) (f)
chimney

chemise (n) (f)
shirt

chemisier (n) (m)
blouse

chenille (n) (f)
caterpillar

cher/chère (adj)
dear (expensive, special)

cheval (n) (m)
horse

chevalier (n) (m)
knight

a
b
Cc
d
e
f
g
h
i
j
k
l
m
n
o
p
q
r
s
t
u
v
w
x
y
z

a
b

Cc

d
e
f
g
h
i
j
k
l
m
n
o
p
q
r
s
t
u
v
w
x
y
z

cheveux (n) (m)
hair

cheville (n) (f)
ankle

chèvre (n) (f)
goat

chewing-gum (n) (m)
chewing gum

chien (n) (m)
dog

chien de berger (n) (m)
sheepdog

chimpanzé (n) (m)
chimpanzee

chiot (n) (m)
puppy

chirurgie (n) (f)
surgery (operation)

chocolat (n) (m)
chocolate

chocolat chaud (n) (m)
hot chocolate

chose (n) (f)
thing

chou (n) (m)
cabbage

chouette (adj)
fun

ciel (n) (m)
sky

cil (n) (m)
eyelash

cinéma (n) (m)
cinema, movie theater

cintre (n) (m)
coat hanger

circulation (n) (f)
traffic

cirque (n) (m)
circus

ciseaux (n) (m)
scissors

citron (n) (m)
lemon

citrouille (n) (f)
pumpkin

clair/claire (adj)
clear, light (not dark)

clavier (n) (m)
keyboard

clé (n) (f)
key

client/cliente (n) (m/f)
customer

cloche (n) (f)
bell

clown (n) (m)
clown

coccinelle (n) (f)
ladybug

cochon (n) (m)
pig

cochon d'Inde (n) (m)
guinea pig

code postal (n) (m)
zip code

cœur (n) (m)
heart

coffre à jouets (n) (m)
toy box

coiffeur/coiffeuse (n) (m/f)
hairdresser

coin (n) (m)
corner

collant/collante (adj)
sticky

collants (n) (m)
tights

colle (n) (f)
glue

collier (n) (m)
collar (dog), necklace

colline (n) (f)
hill

coloré/colorée (adj)
colorful

commandes (n) (f)
controls

comme (prep)
like

comment (adv)
how

commode (n) (f)
chest of drawers

concert (n) (m)
concert

cône de signalisation (n) (m)
traffic cone

confiture (n) (f)
jam

confortable (adj)
comfortable

congélateur (n) (m)
freezer

content/contente (adj)
happy

continent (n) (m)
continent

contraire (n) (m)
opposite

coquillage (n) (m)
shell

corde (n) (f)
rope

corde à sauter (n) (f)
jump rope

corne (n) (f)
horn

corps (n) (m)
body

costume (n) (m)
costume, suit

côte (n) (f)
coast

coton (n) (m)
cotton

cou (n) (m)
neck

coucher de soleil (n) (m)
sunset

coude (n) (m)
elbow

couette (n) (f)
comforter

couleur (n) (f)
color

couloir (n) (m)
hallway

cour de récréation (n) (f)
playground

courageux/courageuse (adj)
brave

courbé (adj)
curved

couronne (n) (f)
crown

courriel (n) (m)
email

course (n) (f)
race

course à pied (n) (f)
running

courses (n) (f)
shopping

court/courte (adj)
short

cousin/cousine (n) (m/f)
cousin

coussin (n) (m)
cushion

couteau (n) (m)
knife

couvercle (n) (m)
lid

couverture (n) (f)
blanket

cow-boy (n) (m)
cowboy

crabe (n) (m)
crab

crapaud (n) (m)
toad

cravate (n) (f)
tie

crayon à papier (n) (m)
pencil

crayon de couleur (n) (m)
colored pencil, crayon

crèche (n) (f)
nursery

crème (n) (f)
cream

crème solaire (n) (f)
sunblock

crêpe (n) (f)
pancake

crocodile (n) (m)
crocodile

cruche (n) (f)
jug

cube (n) (m)
cube

cubes (n) (m)
toy blocks

cuillère (n) (f)
spoon

cuisine (n) (f)
kitchen

cuisinière (n) (f)
stove

curieux/curieuse (adj)
curious

cygne (n) (m)
swan

D

d'abord (adv)
first

d'habitude (adv)
usually

danger (n) (m)
danger

dangereux/dangereuse (adj)
dangerous

dans (prep)
into

danseur/danseuse (n) (m/f)
dancer

danseur/danseuse classique (n) (m/f)
ballet dancer

date (n) (f)
date

dauphin (n) (m)
dolphin

de (prep)
from

de l'autre côté de (prep)
across

dé/dés (n) (m)
dice

décoration (n) (f)
decoration

défi (n) (m)
challenge

défilé (n) (m)
parade

déguisement (n) (m)
costume

dehors (adv)
outside

déjà (adv)
already

déjeuner (n) (m)
lunch

délicieux/délicieuse (adj)
delicious

deltaplane (n) (m)
hang glider

demain (adv)
tomorrow

demi-cercle (n) (m)
semicircle

demi-frère (n) (m)
stepbrother

demi-soeur (n) (f)
stepsister

dent (n) (f)
tooth

dentifrice (n) (m)
toothpaste

dentiste (n) (m/f)
dentist

déplantoir (n) (m)
trowel

dernier/dernière (adj)
last

derrière (prep)
behind

désert (n) (m)
desert

désordre (n) (m)
mess

dessert (n) (m)
dessert

dessin (n) (m)
drawing (act of)

deux fois
twice

deuxième (adj)
second (2nd)

devoirs (n) (m)
homework

diagramme (n) (m)
diagram

dictionnaire (n) (m)
dictionary

Dieu (n) (m)
God

différent/différente (adj)
different

difficile (adj)
difficult

dindon (n) (m)
turkey (bird)

dîner (n) (m)
dinner

dinosaure (n) (m)
dinosaur

directement (adv)
directly

direction (n) (f)
direction

discothèque (n) (f)
disco, nightclub

discours (n) (m)
speech

disque dur (n) (m)
hard drive

distance (n) (f)
distance

divorcé/divorcée (adj)
divorced

doigt (n) (m)
finger

a
b
c

Dd
Ee

f
g
h
i
j
k
l
m
n
o
p
q
r
s
t
u
v
w
x
y
z

dôme (n) (m)
dome

dos (n) (m)
back (body)

doucement (adv)
gently

douche (n) (f)
shower

doux/douce (adj)
gentle, soft

dragon (n) (m)
dragon

drap (n) (m)
bedsheet

drapeau (n) (m)
flag

droit/droite (adj)
straight, right (not left)

dur/dure (adj)
hard, tough

DVD (n) (m)
DVD

E

eau (n) (f)
water

échange (n) (m)
exchange

écharpe (n) (f)
scarf

échecs (n) (m)
chess

échelle (n) (f)
ladder

écho (n) (m)
echo

éclair (n) (m)
lightning

école (n) (f)
school

écran (n) (m)
screen

écriture (n) (f)
writing (act of)

écureuil (n) (m)
squirrel

effet (n) (m)
effect

effrayé/effrayée (adj)
frightened

égal/égale (adj)
equal

église (n) (f)
church

élastique (n) (m)
rubber band

électrique (adj)
electrical

élégant/élégante (adj)
stylish

éléphant (n) (m)
elephant

élève (n) (m/f)
pupil

elle (pron)
she

elles (pron)
they

émission (n) (f)
program (TV)

emploi (n) (m)
job

en arrière (adv)
backward

en avant (adv)
forward

en bois (adj)
wooden

en bonne santé (adj)
healthy

en colère (adj)
angry

en cuir (adj)
leather

en espèces (adv)
(in) cash

en face de (prep)
opposite

en forme (adj)
fit, in shape

en haut (adv)
upstairs

en plastique (adj)
plastic

en retard (adj)
late

en sécurité (adj)
safe

encore (adv)
again

encre (n) (f)
ink

encyclopédie (n) (f)
encyclopedia

endroit (n) (m)
place

**enfant/enfants
(n) (m/f)**
child/children

ennui (n) (m)
trouble, boredom

**ennuyeux/ennuyeuse
(adj)**
boring

ensemble (adv)
together

**ensoleillé/ensoleillée
(adj)**
sunny

enthousiaste (adj)
enthusiastic

entre (prep)
between

entrée (n) (f)
entrance

enveloppe (n) (f)
envelope

environ (adv)
about

environnement (n) (m)
environment

épais/épaisse (adj)
thick

épaule (n) (f)
shoulder

éponge (n) (f)
sponge

épouse (n) (f)
wife

équateur (n) (m)
equator

équipage (n) (m)
crew

équipe (n) (f)
team

équitation (n) (f)
horseback riding

erreur (n) (f)
mistake

escalier (n) (m)
stairs

escargot (n) (m)
snail

espace (n) (m)
space

espagnol (n) (m)
Spanish

essence (n) (f)
gasoline

essuie-tout (n) (m)
paper towel

est (n) (m)
east

estomac (n) (m)
stomach

et (conj)
and

étage (n) (m)
story (building)

étagère (n) (f)
shelf

étang (n) (m)
pond

été (n) (m)
summer

éteint/éteinte (adj)
extinct, turned off

étoile (n) (f)
star

étoile de mer (n) (f)
starfish

étonnant/étonnante (adj)
surprising

étrange (adj)
strange

étranger/étrangère (adj)
foreign

être humain (n) (m)
human being

étroit/étroite (adj)
narrow

événement (n) (m)
event

évier (n) (m)
sink (kitchen)

exact/exacte (adj)
right (correct)

examen (n) (m)
exam

excellent/excellente (adj)
excellent

excité/excitée (adj)
excited

exercice (n) (m)
exercise

expédition (n) (f)
expedition

expérience (n) (f)
experiment

expert/experte (n) (m/f)
expert

explorateur/exploratrice (n) (m/f)
explorer

explosion (n) (f)
explosion

extrêmement (adv)
extremely

F

fabuleux/fabuleuse (adj)
fabulous

facile (adj)
easy

facteur/factrice (n) (m/f)
mail carrier

faible (adj)
faint (pale), weak

fait (n) (m)
fact

falaise (n) (f)
cliff

famille (n) (f)
family

fantastique (adj)
fantastic

farine (n) (f)
flour

fatigué/fatiguée (adj)
tired

faucon (n) (m)
hawk

fauteuil (n) (m)
armchair

fauteuil roulant (n) (m)
wheelchair

faux/fausse (adj)
false

femme (n) (f)
female (human), woman

fenêtre (n) (f)
window

fer à repasser (n) (m)
iron (clothes)

ferme (n) (f)
farm

fermé/fermée (adj)
closed

fermeture éclair (n) (f)
zipper

fermier/fermière (n) (m/f)
farmer

ferry (n) (m)
ferry

fête (n) (f)
festival, party

fête foraine (n) (f)
fairground

feu (n) (m)
fire

feuille (n) (f)
leaf, sheet of paper

feutre (n) (m)
marker

feux de signalisation (n) (m)
traffic lights

ficelle (n) (f)
string

filet (n) (m)
net

fille (n) (f)
daughter, girl

film (n) (m)
film

fin (n) (f)
end (final part)

fin/fine (adj)
thin

flèche (n) (f)
arrow

fleur (n) (f)
flower

flocon de neige (n) (m)
snowflake

flûte (n) (f)
flute

foin (n) (m)
hay

foire (n) (f)
fair

football (n) (m)
soccer

forêt (n) (f)
forest

forêt tropicale (n) (f)
rain forest

forme (n) (f)
shape

formidable (adj)
great

fort/forte (adj)
strong

four (n) (m)
oven

fourchette (n) (f)
fork

fourmi (n) (f)
ant

frais/fraîche (adj)
cool, fresh

fraise (n) (f)
strawberry

a
Bb
c
d
Ee
Ff
g
h
i
j
k
l
m
n
o
p
q
r
s
t
u
v
w
x
y
z

a b c d e

Ff
Gg
Hh

i j k l m n o p q r s t u v w x y z

framboise (n) (f)
raspberry

français (n) (m)
French

frère (n) (m)
brother

frisé/frisée (adj)
curly

frites (n) (f)
fries

froid/froide (adj)
cold

fromage (n) (m)
cheese

fruit (n) (m)
fruit

fruits de mer (n) (m)
seafood

fumée (n) (f)
smoke

fusée (n) (f)
rocket, rocket ship

G

gagnant/gagnante (n) (m/f)
winner

galet (n) (m)
pebble

gant (n) (m)
glove

gant de cuisine (n) (m)
oven mitt

garage (n) (m)
garage

garçon (n) (m)
boy

garçon de café (n) (m)
waiter

gare (n) (f)
train station, station

gâteau (n) (m)
cake

gâteau d'anniversaire (n) (m)
birthday cake

gauche (adj)
left

gaucher/gauchère (adj)
left-handed

gaz (n) (m)
gas (as in stove)

géant (n) (m)
giant

genou (n) (m)
knee

gens (n) (m)
people

gentil/gentille (adj)
kind (gentle)

gilet de sauvetage (n) (m)
life jacket

girafe (n) (f)
giraffe

glace (n) (f)
ice, ice cream

glacier (n) (m)
glacier

glaçon (n) (m)
ice cube

globe (n) (m)
globe

golf (n) (m)
golf

gomme (n) (f)
eraser

gorille (n) (m)
gorilla

goutte (n) (f)
drop

gouvernement (n) (m)
government

graine (n) (f)
seed

grand/grande (adj)
big, tall

grand-mère (n) (f)
grandmother

grand-père (n) (m)
grandfather

grands-parents (n) (m)
grandparents

grange (n) (f)
barn

gratte-ciel (n) (m)
skyscraper

grenier (n) (m)
attic

grenouille (n) (f)
frog

griffe (n) (f)
claw

grille-pain (n) (m)
toaster

gris/grise (adj)
gray

gros/grosse (adj)
big, fat

grotte (n) (f)
cave

groupe (n) (m)
band, group

grue (n) (f)
crane

guépard (n) (m)
cheetah

guêpe (n) (f)
wasp

guerre (n) (f)
war

guide (n) (m)
guide

guitare (n) (f)
guitar

gymnastique (n) (f)
gymnastics

H

habitat (n) (m)
habitat

hamster (n) (m)
hamster

hanche (n) (f)
hip

handicapé/handicapée (adj)
disabled

haricots verts (n) (m)
green beans

haut/haute (adj)
high

hauts-parleurs (n) (m)
speakers

hélicoptère (n) (m)
helicopter (n)

hélicoptère de police (n) (m)
police helicopter

herbe (n) (f)
grass

héron (n) (m)
heron

héros (n) (m)
hero

heure (n) (f)
hour, time

heures d'ouverture (n) (f)
opening hours

hexagone (n) (m)
hexagon

hibou (n) (m)
owl

hier (adv)
yesterday

histoire (n) (f)
history, story

historique (adj)
historical

hiver (n) (m)
winter

hockey (n) (m)
hockey

hockey sur glace (n) (m)
ice hockey

homme (n) (m)
male (human), man

hôpital (n) (m)
hospital

horaire (n) (m)
timetable, schedule

horloge (n) (f)
clock

horrible (adj)
horrible

hors de (prep)
out of

hot-dog (n) (m)
hotdog

hôtel (n) (m)
hotel

huile (n) (f)
oil

I

idée (n) (f)
idea

il (pron)
he

il y a du vent
(it's) windy

île (n) (f)
island

ils (pron)
they

image (n) (f)
picture

immobile (adj)
still

imperméable (n) (m)
raincoat

important/importante (adj)
important

impossible (adj)
impossible

incroyable (adj)
amazing

infirmier/infirmière (n) (m/f)
nurse

information (n) (f)
information

ingrédient (n) (m)
ingredient

inhabituel/inhabituelle (adj)
unusual

injuste (adj)
unfair

inondation (n) (f)
flood

insecte (n) (m)
insect

instruction (n) (f)
instruction

instrument (n) (m)
instrument

intelligent/intelligente (adj)
clever

intéressant/intéressante (adj)
interesting

international/internationale (adj)
international

Internet (n) (m)
Internet

invitation (n) (f)
invitation

J

jamais (adv)
never

jambe (n) (f)
leg

jardin (n) (m)
garden

jardinage (n) (m)
gardening

jardinier/jardinière (n) (m/f)
gardener

jaune (adj)
yellow

je/j' (pron)
I

jean (n) (m)
jeans

jeu (n) (m)
game

jeu de société (n) (m)
board game

jeu électronique (n) (m)
electronic game

jeu vidéo (n) (m)
video game (n)

jeune (adj)
young

Jeux Olympiques (n) (m)
Olympic Games

joli/jolie (adj)
pretty

jouet (n) (m)
toy

joueur/joueuse (n) (m/f)
player

jour (n) (m)
day

journal (n) (m)
diary, newspaper

judo (n) (m)
judo

jumeau/jumelle (n) (m/f)
twin

jumelles (n) (f)
binoculars

jungle (n) (f)
jungle

jupe (n) (f)
skirt

jus (n) (m)
juice

jus d'orange (n) (m)
orange juice

jusqu'à (prep)
until

juste (adj)
correct

juste (adv)
just

a
b
c
d
e
f
g
Hh
Ii
Jj
k
l
m
n
o
p
q
r
s
t
u
v
w
x
y
z

a
b
c
d
e
f
g
h
i
j

Kk
Ll
Mm

n
o
p
q
r
s
t
u
v
w
x
y
z

K

kangourou (n) (m)
kangaroo

karaté (n) (m)
karate

koala (n) (m)
koala

L

la/lui/l' (pron)
her

là (adv)
there

là-bas (adv)
over there

lac (n) (m)
lake

laid/laide (adj)
ugly

laine (n) (f)
wool

lait (n) (m)
milk

**laitier/laitière
(adj)**
dairy

laitue (n) (f)
lettuce

lampe (n) (f)
lamp

lampe de poche (n) (f)
flashlight

langue (n) (f)
language, tongue

lapin (n) (m)
rabbit

large (adj)
loose, wide

lavabo (n) (m)
sink (bathroom)

le/lui/l' (pron)
him

le/la/l'/les (article)
the

le sien/la sienne (pron)
his/hers

leçon (n) (f)
lesson

**lecteur de DVD
(n) (m)**
DVD player

lecteur MP3 (n) (m)
MP3 player

lecture (n) (f)
reading

léger/légère (adj)
light (not heavy)

légume (n) (m)
vegetable

lent/lente (adj)
slow

lentement (adv)
slowly

léopard (n) (m)
leopard

lettre (n) (f)
letter (alphabet, mail)

leur (adj)
their

lézard (n) (m)
lizard

libellule (n) (f)
dragonfly

liberté (n) (f)
freedom

librairie (n) (f)
bookstore

lièvre (n) (m)
hare

ligne (n) (f)
line

limonade (n) (f)
lemonade

lion (n) (m)
lion

liquide (n) (m)
liquid (n)

lisse (adj)
smooth

liste (n) (f)
list

liste de courses (n) (f)
shopping list

lit (n) (m)
bed

livre (n) (m)
book

loi (n) (f)
law

loin (adv)
far

loisir (n) (m)
hobby

long/longue (adj)
long

losange (n) (m)
diamond (shape)

loup (n) (m)
wolf

loupe (n) (f)
magnifying glass

lourd/lourde (adj)
heavy

luge (n) (f)
sledge

lumière (n) (f)
light

lune (n) (f)
moon

lunettes (n) (f)
glasses

**lunettes de natation
(n) (f)**
goggles

**lunettes de soleil
(n) (f)**
sunglasses

M

machine (n) (f)
machine

**machine à laver
(n) (f)**
washing machine

magasin (n) (m)
store

magazine (n) (m)
magazine

**magicien/magicienne
(n) (m/f)**
magician

magnétique (adj)
magnetic

**maillot de bain
(n) (m)**
swimsuit, trunks

main (n) (f)
hand

**maintenant
(adv)**
now

mais (conj)
but

maison (n) (f)
home, house

maître/maîtresse (n) (m/f)
teacher (elementary school)

mal de tête (n) (m)
headache

malade (adj)
ill, sick

maladie (n) (f)
illness

maman (n) (f)
mom

mammifère (n) (m)
mammal

manche (n) (f)
sleeve

manchot (n) (m)
penguin

manteau (n) (m)
coat

maquillage (n) (m)
makeup

marché (n) (m)
market

marée (n) (f)
tide

mari (n) (m)
husband

marié/mariée (adj)
married

marin (n) (m)
sailor

marionnette (n) (f)
puppet

marron (adj)
brown

masque (n) (m)
mask

match (n) (m)
match (sports)

matériel (n) (m)
equipment

mathématiques (n) (f)
math

matin (n) (m)
morning

mauvais/mauvaise (adj)
bad

mauvaise herbe (n) (f)
weed

me/moi/m' (pron)
me

médecin (n) (m)
doctor

médicament (n) (m)
medicine

méduse (n) (f)
jellyfish

meilleur/meilleure (adj)
better

mélange (n) (m)
mixture

melon (n) (m)
melon

même (adv)
even

même (adj)
same

menton (n) (m)
chin

mer (n) (f)
sea

mère (n) (f)
mother

message (n) (m)
message

mesure (n) (f)
measurement

mètre (n) (m)
tape measure

métro (n) (m)
subway

meubles (n) (m)
furniture

micro-ondes (n) (m)
microwave

miel (n) (m)
honey

mieux (adj)
best

milieu (n) (m)
middle

milk-shake (n) (m)
milkshake

mille
thousand

milliard
billion

million
million

minéral (n) (m)
mineral

minuit (n) (m)
midnight

minuscule (adj)
tiny

minute (n) (f)
minute

miroir (n) (m)
mirror

mitaine (n) (f)
mitten

mode (n) (f)
fashion

mois (n) (m)
month

moisson (n) (f)
harvest

moissonneuse-batteuse (n) (f)
combine harvester

moitié (n) (f)
half

mon/ma (adj)
my

monde (n) (m)
world

monstre (n) (m)
monster

montagne (n) (f)
mountain

montgolfière (n) (f)
hot-air balloon

montre (n) (f)
watch

moquette (n) (f)
carpet

morceau (n) (m)
piece

mort/morte (adj)
dead

mosquée (n) (f)
mosque

mot (n) (m)
term, word

moteur (n) (m)
motor

motif (n) (m)
pattern

moto (n) (f)
motorcycle

mouche (n) (f)
fly

mouchoir (n) (m)
handkerchief

mouchoirs en papier (n) (m)
tissues

mouette (n) (f)
seagull

mouillé/mouillée (adj)
wet

moustache (n) (f)
mustache, whisker

a b c d e f g h i j k l **Mm** n o p q r s t u v w x y z

105

a
b
c
d
e
f
g
h
i
j
k
l

Mm
Nn
Oo

p
q
r
s
t
u
v
w
x
y
z

mouton (n) (m)
sheep

mur (n) (m)
wall

mûr/mûre (adj)
ripe

musée (n) (m)
museum

musicien/musicienne (n) (m/f)
musician

musique (n) (f)
music

N

n'importe qui (pron)
anybody

n'importe quoi (pron)
anything

nageoire (n) (f)
fin

natation (n) (f)
swimming

nature (n) (f)
nature

navire (n) (m)
ship

neige (n) (f)
snow

nénuphar (n) (m)
water lily

neveu (n) (m)
nephew

nez (n) (m)
nose

nid (n) (m)
nest

nièce (n) (f)
niece

Noël (n) (m)
Christmas

nœud (n) (m)
knot

noir/noire (adj)
black

nom (n) (m)
name

nombre (n) (m)
number

nord (n) (m)
north

note (n) (f)
mark, grade

notre (adj)
our

nouilles (n) (f)
noodles

nourriture (n) (f)
food

nous (pron)
we

nouveau/nouvelle (adj)
new

nouvelles (n) (f)
news

nuage (n) (m)
cloud

nuageux/nuageuse (adj)
cloudy

nuit (n) (f)
night

nulle part (adv)
nowhere

numérique (adj)
digital

O

objet (n) (m)
object

occupé/occupée (adj)
busy

océan (n) (m)
ocean

odeur (n) (f)
smell

œil (n) (m)
eye

œuf (n) (m)
egg

oignon (n) (m)
onion

oiseau (n) (m)
bird

oiseau-mouche (n) (m)
hummingbird

ombre (n) (f)
shadow

oncle (n) (m)
uncle

ongle (n) (m)
nail

opération (n) (f)
operation

or (n) (m)
gold

orage (n) (m)
thunderstorm

orageux/orageuse (adj)
stormy

orange (adj)
orange (color)

orange (n) (f)
orange (fruit)

orchestre (n) (m)
orchestra

ordinateur (n) (m)
computer

ordinateur portable (n) (m)
laptop

ordures (n) (f)
garbage

oreille (n) (f)
ear

oreiller (n) (m)
pillow

orteil (n) (m)
toe

os (n) (m)
bone

otarie (n) (f)
sea lion

otite (n) (f)
earache

ou (conj)
or

où (adv)
where

ouest (n) (m)
west

ouragan (n) (m)
hurricane

ours (n) (m)
bear

ours blanc (n) (m)
polar bear

ours en peluche (n) (m)
teddy bear

outil (n) (m)
tool

ouvert/ouverte (adj)
open

ovale (n) (m)
oval

P

page (n) (f)
page

paille (n) (f)
straw

pain (n) (m)
bread

paire (n) (f)
pair

paix (n) (f)
peace

palme (n) (f)
flipper

palmier (n) (m)
palm tree

panda (n) (m)
panda

panier (n) (m)
basket

panneau (n) (m)
sign

pantalon (n) (m)
pants

pantoufle (n) (f)
slipper

papa (n) (m)
dad

papier (n) (m)
paper

papier toilette (n) (m)
toilet paper

papillon (n) (m)
butterfly

papillon de nuit (n) (m)
moth

pâquerette (n) (f)
daisy

parapluie (n) (m)
umbrella (for rain)

parasol (n) (m)
umbrella (for sun)

parc (n) (m)
park

parce que (conj)
because

parent (n) (m)
parent

paresseux/paresseuse (adj)
lazy

parfait/parfaite (adj)
perfect

particulier/particulière (adj)
special

partie (n) (f)
part

partout (adv)
everywhere

pas (n) (m)
step

passage clouté (n) (m)
crosswalk

passager/passagère (n) (m/f)
passenger

passé (n) (m)
past (history)

passeport (n) (m)
passport

pastèque (n) (f)
watermelon

pâte à modeler (n) (f)
modeling clay

pâtes (n) (f)
pasta

patient/patiente (adj)
patient

patient/patiente (n) (m/f)
patient

patinage sur glace (n) (m)
ice-skating

patte (n) (f)
foot (animal), paw

pause (n) (f)
break (pause)

pauvre (adj)
poor

pays (n) (m)
country

peau (n) (f)
skin, peel

pêche (n) (f)
fishing, peach

pédale (n) (f)
pedal

peigne (n) (m)
comb

peinture (n) (f)
paint

pélican (n) (m)
pelican

pelle (n) (f)
shovel

pelouse (n) (f)
lawn

pendant (prep)
during

pendant que (conj)
while

pentagone (n) (m)
pentagon

père (n) (m)
father

perle (n) (f)
bead

perroquet (n) (m)
parrot

personne (pron)
nobody

personne (n) (f)
person

personne âgée (n) (f)
old person

petit/petite (adj)
little, small

petit ami (m)
boyfriend

petit-déjeuner (n) (m)
breakfast

petit pain (m)
(bread) roll

petit pois (m)
pea

petit tapis (m)
mat

petite amie (f)
girlfriend

peu profond/peu profonde (adj)
shallow

peut-être (adv)
maybe, perhaps

phare (n) (m)
lighthouse

pharmacie (n) (f)
pharmacy

phoque (n) (m)
seal

photo (n) (f)
photo

piano (n) (m)
piano

pièce (n) (f)
coin, room

pièce de théâtre (n) (f)
play

pied (n) (m)
foot

pierre (n) (f)
stone

a
b
c
d
e
f
g
h
i
j
k
l
m
n
o
Pp
q
r
s
t
u
v
w
x
y
z

pile (n) (f)
battery

pilote (n) (m)
pilot

pin (n) (m)
pine tree

pinceau (n) (m)
paint brush

pique-nique (n) (m)
picnic

pire (adj)
worst

piscine (n) (f)
swimming pool

pissenlit (n) (m)
dandelion

pizza (n) (f)
pizza

placard (n) (m)
cupboard

plafond (n) (m)
ceiling

plage (n) (f)
beach

planche de surf (n) (f)
surfboard

planète (n) (f)
planet

plante (n) (f)
plant

plat/plate (adj)
flat, level

plateau (n) (m)
tray

plein/pleine (adj)
full

plongée (n) (f)
diving

pluie (n) (f)
rain

plume (n) (f)
feather

plus que
more than

pneu (n) (m)
tire

poche (n) (f)
pocket

poêle (n) (f)
frying pan

poils (n) (m)
fur

poilu/poilue (adj)
hairy

point (n) (m)
point

poire (n) (f)
pear

poisson (n) (m)
fish

poisson rouge (n) (m)
goldfish

poitrine (n) (f)
chest

poivre (n) (m)
pepper

polaire (n) (f)
fleece

police (n) (f)
police

pomme (n) (f)
apple

pomme de pin (n) (f)
pinecone

pomme de terre (n) (f)
potato

pompier (n) (m)
firefighter

pont (n) (m)
bridge, deck (boat)

populaire (adj)
popular

port (n) (m)
harbor

porte (n) (f)
door

porte d'entrée (n) (f)
front door

porte-monnaie (n) (m)
wallet, purse

possible (adj)
possible

poste (n) (f)
mail

pot de peinture (n) (m)
paint can

poteau (n) (m)
pole

poubelle (n) (f)
trash can

pouce (n) (m)
thumb

poudre (n) (f)
powder

poulet (n) (m)
chicken (meat)

poupée (n) (f)
doll

pourquoi (adv)
why

poussette (n) (f)
stroller

poussière (n) (f)
dust

poussin (n) (m)
chick

préféré/préférée (adj)
favorite

premier/première (adj)
first

premiers secours (n) (m)
first aid

près de (prep)
near

président/e (n) (m/f)
president

presque (adv)
almost, nearly

prêt/prête (adj)
ready

prince (n) (m)
prince

princesse (n) (f)
princess

principal/principale (adj)
main

printemps (n) (m)
spring (season)

prise électrique (n) (f)
plug (electric)

prix (n) (m)
price, prize

probablement (adv)
probably

problème (n) (m)
problem

prochain/prochaine (adj)
next

proche (adj)
close (near)

profond/profonde (adj)
deep

projet (n) (m)
project

promenade (n) (f)
walk

propre (adj)
clean, own

prudent/prudente (adj)
careful

pull (n) (m)
sweater

punaise (n) (f)
thumbtack

puzzle (n) (m)
puzzle

pyjama (n) (m)
pajamas

a
b
c
d
e
f
g
h
i
j
k
l
m
n
o

Pp

q
r
s
t
u
v
w
x
y
z

Q

quai (n) (m)
platform

quand (adv)
when

quart (n) (m)
quarter

**quelque chose
(pron)**
something

quelquefois (adv)
sometimes

quelques (adj)
some

quelqu'un (pron)
someone

question (n) (f)
question

queue (n) (f)
line, tail

qui (pron)
who

quiz (n) (m)
quiz

R

racine (n) (f)
root

radio (n) (f)
radio

raide (adj)
steep, stiff

raisin (n) (m)
grape

rame (n) (f)
oar

rapide (adj)
fast

raquette (n) (f)
racket

rat (n) (m)
rat

râteau (n) (m)
rake

rayures (n) (f)
stripes

recette (n) (f)
recipe

récolte (n) (f)
crop

récréation (n) (f)
playtime

rectangle (n) (m)
rectangle

réel/réelle (adj)
real

réfrigérateur (n) (m)
refrigerator

région (n) (f)
area

règle (n) (f)
ruler (measuring)

reine (n) (f)
queen

renard (n) (m)
fox

repas (n) (m)
meal

réponse (n) (f)
answer

requin (n) (m)
shark

restaurant (n) (m)
restaurant

rêve (n) (m)
dream

réveil (n) (m)
alarm clock

réverbère (n) (m)
streetlight

rhinocéros (n) (m)
rhinoceros

riche (adj)
rich

rideau (n) (m)
curtain

rien (pron)
nothing

rive (n) (f)
bank (river)

rivière (n) (f)
river

riz (n) (m)
rice

robe (n) (f)
dress

robinet (n) (m)
faucet

robot (n) (m)
robot

rocher (n) (m)
rock

roi (n) (m)
king

rond/ronde (adj)
round

rose (adj)
pink

rose (n) (f)
rose

roue (n) (f)
wheel

rouge (adj)
red

route (n) (f)
road

ruban (n) (m)
ribbon

ruche (n) (f)
hive

rue (n) (f)
street

rugby (n) (m)
rugby

rugueux/rugueuse (adj)
rough

S

**s'il te plaît/s'il vous
plaît (formal)**
please

sable (n) (m)
sand

sac (n) (m)
bag, sack, shopping bag

sac à dos (n) (m)
backpack

**sac à main
(n) (m)**
handbag, purse

**sac de couchage
(n) (m)**
sleeping bag

**sac en plastique
(n) (m)**
plastic bag

saison (n) (f)
season

salade (n) (f)
salad

salaire (n) (m)
pay

sale (adj)
dirty

a
b
c
d
e
f
g
h
i
j
k
l
m
n
o
p
Qq
Rr
Ss
t
u
v
w
x
y
z

salle à manger (n) (f)
dining room

salle de bains (n) (f)
bathroom

salle de classe (n) (f)
classroom

salon (n) (m)
living room

salut
hi

sandale (n) (f)
sandal

sandwich (n) (m)
sandwich

sang (n) (m)
blood

sans (prep)
without

sauterelle (n) (f)
grasshopper

savon (n) (m)
soap

scarabée (n) (m)
beetle

sciences (n) (f)
science

scientifique (n) (m/f)
scientist

score (n) (m)
score

seau (n) (m)
bucket

sec/sèche (adj)
dry

secours (n) (m)
rescue

sel (n) (m)
salt

selle (n) (f)
saddle

semaine (n) (f)
week

sens (n) (m)
meaning

séparément (adv)
separately

serpent (n) (m)
snake

serre (n) (f)
greenhouse

serré/serrée (adj)
tight

serveuse (n) (f)
waitress

serviette (n) (f)
towel

serviette de toilette (n) (f)
washcloth

seul/seule (adj)
alone

seulement (adv)
only

sévère (adj)
strict

shampooing (n) (m)
shampoo

short (n) (m)
shorts

sien/sienne (pron) (m/f)
his/her

sifflement (n) (m)
whistle

silencieux/silencieuse (adj)
quiet

singe (n) (m)
monkey

site web (n) (m)
website

skate-board (n) (m)
skateboard

ski (n) (m)
skiing

smartphone (n) (m)
smartphone

snowboard (n) (m)
snowboard

sœur (n) (f)
sister

soir (n) (m)
evening

sol (n) (m)
floor

soldat (n) (m)
soldier

soleil (n) (m)
sun

solide (n) (m)
solid

sombre (adj)
dark

son/sa (adj)
her/his/its

sorte (n) (f)
kind (type)

sortie (n) (f)
exit

sourcil (n) (m)
eyebrow

sourd/sourde (adj)
deaf

souris (n) (f)
mouse (animal, computer)

sous (prep)
under

sous-marin (n) (m)
submarine

sous-vêtements (n) (m)
underwear

souvenir (n) (m)
souvenir

souvent (adv)
often

spaghettis (n) (m)
spaghetti

spectacle (n) (m)
show

sphère (n) (m)
sphere

sport (n) (m)
sport

squelette (n) (m)
skeleton

stupide (adj)
stupid

stylo (n) (m)
pen

sucre (n) (m)
sugar

sud (n) (m)
south

sujet (n) (m)
subject

supermarché (n) (m)
supermarket

supplémentaire (adj)
extra

sur (prep)
about, on top of

sûr/sûre (adj)
sure

surf (n) (m)
surfing

surface (n) (f)
surface

surprise (n) (f)
surprise

surveillant de baignade (n) (m)
lifeguard

sympathique (adj)
nice

T

table (n) (f)
table

tableau (n) (m)
picture

tableau noir (n) (m)
blackboard

tablier (n) (m)
apron

taches (n) (f)
spots

taille (n) (f)
size, waist

tante (n) (f)
aunt

tapis (n) (m)
rug

tasse (n) (m)
cup, mug

taxi (n) (m)
taxi

tee-shirt (n) (m)
T-shirt

télécommande (n) (f)
remote control

téléphone (n) (m)
telephone (n)

téléphone portable (n) (m)
cell phone

télescope (n) (m)
telescope

télévision (n) (f)
television

temps (n) (m)
time, weather

temps libre (n) (m)
free time

tennis (n) (m)
tennis

tennis de table (n) (m)
ping-pong

tente (n) (f)
tent

terrain (n) (m)
land

Terre (n) (f)
Earth (planet)

terre (n) (f)
ground, soil

terrible (adj)
terrible

têtard (n) (m)
tadpole

tête (n) (f)
head

texto (n) (m)
text message

thé (n) (m)
tea

thermomètre (n) (m)
thermometer

ticket de caisse (n) (m)
receipt

tige (n) (f)
stem

tigre (n) (m)
tiger

timbre (n) (m)
stamp

timide (adj)
shy

tiroir (n) (m)
drawer

tissu (n) (m)
cloth

toboggan aquatique (n) (m)
waterslide

toilettes (n) (f)
toilet

toit (n) (m)
roof

tomate (n) (f)
tomato

tondeuse à gazon (n) (f)
lawn mower

torchon (n) (m)
dish towel

tornade (n) (f)
tornado

tortue (n) (f)
tortoise

tortue de mer (n) (f)
turtle

tôt (adv)
early

toucan (n) (m)
toucan

toujours (adv)
always

touriste (n) (m/f)
tourist

tournant (n) (m)
turn (bend)

tournesol (n) (m)
sunflower

tourniquet (n) (m)
merry-go-round

tous (adj)
every

tous les jours (adv)
every day

tout (pron)
everything

tout/toute (adj)
all

tout à coup (adv)
suddenly

tout de suite (adv)
immediately

tout le monde (pron)
everybody

toux (n) (f)
cough

tracteur (n) (m)
tractor

train (n) (m)
train, train set

traîneau (n) (m)
sleigh

trajet (n) (m)
route

tranquille (adj)
peaceful

tranquillement (adv)
quietly

transport (n) (m)
transportation

très (adv)
very

triangle (n) (m)
triangle

triste (adj)
sad

troisième (adj)
third

trombone (n) (m)
paper clip

trompe (n) (f)
trunk (animal)

tronc (n) (m)
trunk (tree)

tropical/tropicale (adj)
tropical

trottoir (n) (m)
sidewalk

trou (n) (m)
hole

troupeau (n) (m)
flock (of sheep)

trousse (n) (f)
pencil case

a
b
c
d
e
f
g
h
i
j
k
l
m
n
o
p
q
r
s
Tt
u
v
w
x
y
z

tu/vous (pron)
you

tube (n) (m)
tube

tunnel (n) (m)
tunnel

U

un/une (article)
a, an

uniforme (n) (m)
uniform

uniforme scolaire (n) (m)
school uniform

univers (n) (m)
universe

urgence (n) (f)
emergency

usine (n) (f)
factory

utile (adj)
useful

V

vacances (n) (f)
vacation

vache (n) (f)
cow

vague (n) (f)
wave

vaisselle (n) (f)
(doing the) dishes

valise (n) (f)
suitcase

veau (n) (m)
calf

vedette de cinéma (n) (f)
movie star

végétarien/ végétarienne (n) (m/f)
vegetarian

vélo (n) (m)
bicycle

vendeur/vendeuse (n) (m/f)
salesclerk

vent (n) (m)
wind

ventre (n) (m)
tummy

ver (n) (m)
worm

ver de terre (n) (m)
earthworm

verbe (n) (m)
verb

verre (n) (m)
glass (drink)

vers (prep)
toward

vert/verte (adj)
green

vêtements (n) (m)
clothes

vétérinaire (n) (m/f)
vet

viande (n) (f)
meat

vide (adj)
empty

vie (n) (f)
life

vieux/vieille (adj)
old

vilain/vilaine (adj)
naughty

village (n) (m)
village

ville (n) (f)
city, town

violet/violette (adj)
purple

violon (n) (m)
violin

visage (n) (m)
face

vite (adv)
quickly

voile (n) (f)
sail

voisin/voisine (n) (m/f)
neighbor

voiture (n) (f)
car

voiture de course (n) (f)
race car

voiture de police (n) (f)
police car

votre (adj)
your

voyage (n) (m)
journey, trip

vrai/vraie (adj)
true

vraiment (adv)
really

V. T. T. (vélo tout terrain) (n) (m)
mountain bike

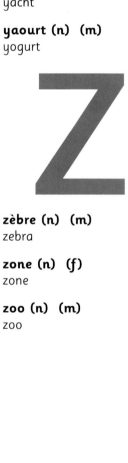

W

Y

week-end (n) (m)
weekend

yacht (n) (m)
yacht

yaourt (n) (m)
yogurt

Z

zèbre (n) (m)
zebra

zone (n) (f)
zone

zoo (n) (m)
zoo

Tt
Uu
Vv
Ww
x
Yy
Zz

Speaking French

In this dictionary, we have spelled out each French word in a way that will help you pronounce it. Use this guide to help you understand how the word should sound when you say it. Some French words look the same as English but sound very different!

When speaking French, the stress of each word is on the last syllable, so you say it a little bit louder. Each syllable is spoken for the same amount of time.

Letter	Pronunciation	Our spelling	Example
a, à, â	between the *a* in h*a*t and f*a*r	*a* or *ah*	**adresse** *a-dreys*
ch	like *sh* in *sh*ip	*sh*	**changer** *shahn-zhay*
ç	like *s* in *s*it	*s*	**garçon** *gar-so(n)*
é	like *ay* in d*ay*	*ay*	**café** *ka-fay*
è, ê	like *e* in m*e*t	*eh*	**crème** *krehm*
e	like *er* in oth*er*	*uh*	**de** *duh*
gn	like the *ni* in o*ni*on	*nye* or *n-ye*	**ligne** *leen-ye*
i, y	like *ee* in f*ee*t	*ee*	**fille** *fee-ye*
j and sometimes g	like *s* in mea*s*ure	*zh*	**bonjour** *bon-zhoor*
qu	like *k* in *k*ing	*k*	**queue** *kuh*
o, ô	like *o* in m*o*re	*o* or *oh*	**porte** *port*
r	say *ruh* at the back of your throat, as if you're gargling	*r*	**fleur** *fluhr*
u	like *ew* in f*ew*	*ew*	**tu** *tew*
an, en, ien, in, ain, ein, on, un am, em, im, aim, eim, om, um	the *n* is not pronounced, but the vowel in front of it should have a nasal sound, as if the word ended in *ng*; for example, as if you said *song*, but stopped before saying the final *ng*.	*a(n), ah(n), o(n)*	**bien** *bya(n)*

113

Verbs

This section gives a list of useful verbs (doing words). They are all in the infinitive form (to...). The most useful verbs, such as "to be" (*être*) and "to have" (*avoir*), are written out so that you can see how they change depending on who is doing the action. I = *je*, you = *tu*, he/she = *il/elle*, we = *nous*, you (plural and formal) = *vous*, and they = *ils/elles*.

We have also written out three of the most regular French verbs—to give (*donner*), to finish (*finir*), and to sell (*vendre*)—so you can see how these change. There is also a reflexive verb written out. Reflexive verbs are often used when you would say "myself" or "yourself" in English. One example is "to wash oneself" (*se laver*).

to act
faire du théâtre
fair dew tay-a-truh

to agree
être d'accord
eh-truh da-kor

to allow
permettre
pair-met-truh

to appear
apparaître
ap-par-eh-truh

to ask
demander
duh-mahn-day

to bake
faire des gâteaux
fair day gah-to

to bark
aboyer
ab-wa-yay

to be
être
eh-truh

I am
je suis
zhuh swee

you are
tu es
tew eh

he, she is
il, elle est
eel/el eh

we are
nous sommes
noo som

you (plural) are
vous êtes
voo-zet

they are
ils, elles sont
el soh(n)

to be able
pouvoir
poov-wahr

to be born
être né
eh-truh nay

to be called
être appelé
eh-truh ap-play

to be cold
avoir froid
av-wahr frwa

to be hungry
avoir faim
av-wahr fa(m)

to be scared of
avoir peur de
av-wahr puhr duh

Je fais des gâteaux.
I am **baking**.

Simon **croque** une pomme.
Simon is **biting** an apple.

Elle **gonfle** un ballon.
She **blows** up a balloon.

Luc **nettoie** le sol.
Luc **cleans** the floor.

to be thirsty
avoir soif
av-wahr swaf

to become
devenir
duh-vuh-neer

to begin
commencer
ko-mah(n)-say

to behave
se comporter
suh kom-por-tay

to believe
croire
krwahr

to bend
plier
plee-yay

to bird-watch
observer les oiseaux
ob-zair-vay layz-wa-zoh

to bite
croquer
kro-kay

to block
bloquer
blo-kay

to blow
gonfler
gon-flay

to boil
bouillir
boo-yeer

to borrow
emprunter
ahm-pran-tay

to bounce
rebondir
ruh-bon-deer

to brake
freiner
fray-nay

to break
casser
kah-say

to breathe
respirer
res-pee-ray

to bring
apporter
ap-por-tay

to brush
brosser
bro-say

**to brush
one's teeth**
se brosser les dents
suh bro-say lay dah(n)

to build
construire
kons-trweer

to bump into
rentrer dans
rahn-tray dah(n)

to buy
acheter
ash-tay

to camp
camper
kahm-pay

to carry
porter
por-tay

to catch
attraper
a-tra-pay

to cause
causer
koh-zay

to celebrate
célébrer
say-lay-bray

to change
changer
shahn-zhay

to charge (a phone)
recharger
ruh-shar-zhay

to check
vérifier
veh-reef-yay

to choose
choisir
shwa-zeer

to clean
nettoyer
neh-twa-yay

to clear (a table)
débarrasser
day-bar-ra-say

to climb
grimper
gram-pay

to close
fermer
fair-may

to code
coder
ko-day

to collect
collectionner
ko-lek-syo-nay

to come
venir
vuh-neer

to come back
revenir
ruh-vuh-neer

to come from
venir de
vuh-neer duh

Attrape le ballon !
Catch the ball!

a
b

Cc
Dd

e
f
g
h
i
j
k
l
m
n
o
p
q
r
s
t
u
v
w
x
y
z

to compare
comparer
kom-pa-ray

to complain
se plaindre
suh plan-druh

to contain
contenir
kon-tuh-neer

to continue
continuer
kon-tee-new-ay

to cook
cuisiner
kwee-zee-nay

to copy
copier
ko-pee-yay

to cost
coûter
koo-tay

to count
compter
kom-tay

to cover
couvrir
koov-reer

to crack
casser
kass-say

to crash
s'écraser
say-krah-zay

to create
créer
kray-ay

to cross
traverser
tra-vair-say

to cry
pleurer
pluhr-ay

to cut
couper
koo-pay

to cut out
découper
day-koo-pay

to cycle
faire du vélo
fair dew vay-lo

to dance
danser
dahn-say

to decide
décider
day-see-day

to decorate
décorer
day-ko-ray

to describe
décrire
day-kreer

to destroy
détruire
day-trweer

to die
mourir
moo-reer

to dig
creuser
kruh-zay

to disappear
disparaître
dees-pa-reh-truh

to discover
découvrir
day-koov-reer

to dive
plonger
plon-jay

to do
faire
fair

I do
je fais
zhuh fay

you do
tu fais
tew fay

he/she does
il/elle fait
eel/el fay

we do
nous faisons
noo fuh-zoh(n)

you (plural) do
vous faites
voo feht

they do
ils/elles font
eel/el foh(n)

to garden
jardiner
zhar-dee-nay

to draw
dessiner
deh-see-nay

Marie **danse** bien.
Marie **dances** well.

Caroline **creuse** dans le sable.
Caroline is **digging** in the sand.

*Stéphane **dessine**.*
*Stéphane **draws**.*

to dream
rêver
reh-vay

to dress up
s'habiller
sa-bee-yay

to drink
boire
bwahr

to drive
conduire
kon-dweer

to dry
sécher
say-shay

to earn
gagner
gan-yay

to eat
manger
mahn-zhay

to encourage
encourager
ahn-koo-ra-zhay

to enjoy
aimer
eh-may

to escape
s'échapper
say-shap-pay

to explain
expliquer
eks-plee-kay

to explode
exploser
ex-ploh-zay

to face
affronter
af-fron-tay

to fall
tomber
tom-bay

to fall down
s'écrouler
say-kroo-lay

to feed
nourrir
noo-reer

to feel
ressentir
ruh-sahn-teer

to fetch
aller chercher
al-lay shair-shay

to fight
se battre
suh bat-truh

to fill
remplir
rahm-pleer

to find
trouver
troo-vay

to find out
se renseigner sur
suh rahn-sen-yay soor

to finish
finir
fee-neer

I finish
je finis
zhuh fee-nee

you finish
tu finis
tew fee-nee

he/she finishes
il/elle finit
eel/el fee-nee

we finish
nous finissons
noo fee-nee-so(n)

you (plural) finish
vous finissez
voo fee-nee-say

they finish
ils/elles finissent
eel/el fee-nees

to float
flotter
flo-tay

a
b
c
Dd
Ee
Ff
g
h
i
j
k
l
m
n
o
p
q
r
s
t
u
v
w
x
y
z

*Je **mange** un gâteau au chocolat.*
*I am **eating** a chocolate cake.*

*Il faut **nourrir** les chiens !*
*We must **feed** the dogs!*

117

a
b
c
d
e

Ff
Gg
Hh

i
j
k
l
m
n
o
p
q
r
s
t
u
v
w
x
y
z

to fly
voler
vo-lay

to fold
plier
plee-yay

to follow
suivre
sweev-ruh

to forget
oublier
oo-blee-yay

to freeze
geler
zhuh-lay

to frighten
effrayer
eh-fray-yay

to get
recevoir
ruh-suhv-wahr

to get on (a bus)
monter
mon-tay

to get ready
se préparer
suh pray-pa-ray

to get up
se lever
suh le-vay

to give
donner
don-nay

I give
je donne
zhuh don

you give
tu donnes
tew don

he/she gives
il/elle donne
eel/el don

we give
nous donnons
noo doh-no(n)

you (plural) give
vous donnez
voo doh-nay

they give
ils/elles donnent
eel/el don

to go
aller
ah-lay

I go
je vais
zhuh vay

you go
tu vas
tew vah

he/she goes
il/elle va
eel/el vah

we go
nous allons
noo-zah-lo(n)

you (plural) go
vous allez
voo-zah-lay

they go
ils/elles vont
eel/el voh(n)

to go camping
faire du camping
fair dew kahm-peeng

to go on vacation
partir en vacances
par-teer ah(n) vak-ahns

to go out
sortir
sor-teer

to go shopping
faire les courses
fair lay koorss

to grow
pousser
poo-say

to guess
deviner
duh-vee-nay

to hang up (a phone)
raccrocher
rah-kro-shay

to happen
arriver
ar-ree-vay

to hate
détester
day-tes-tay

to have
avoir
av-wahr

I have
j'ai
zhay

you have
tu as
tew ah

he/she has
il/elle a
eel/el ah

we have
nous avons
noo-zah-voh(n)

you (plural) have
vous avez
voo-zah-vay

Plie le papier.
Fold the paper.

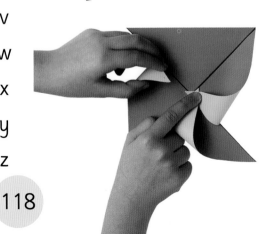

Bruno **prend** des œufs pour **le petit-déjeuner**.
Bruno **has** eggs for **breakfast**.

118

they have
ils/elles ont
eel/el zoh(n)

to have a shower
prendre unedouche
prahn-druh ewn doosh

to have breakfast
prendre le
petit-déjeuner
prahn-druh luh
puh-tee
day-zhuh-nay

to have fun
s'amuser
sah-mew-zay

to have to
devoir
duhv-wahr

to hear
entendre
ahn-tahn-druh

to help
aider
eh-day

to hide
cacher
ka-shay

to hit
frapper
frap-pay

to hold
tenir
tuh-neer

to hop
sauter
soh-tay

to hope
espérer
es-pair-ay

to hurry
se dépêcher
suh day-peh-shay

to hurt
blesser
bleh-say

to imagine
imaginer
ee-ma-zhee-nay

to include
inclure
an-klewr

to inspire
inspirer
an-spee-ray

to invent
inventer
an-vahn-tay

to invite
inviter
an-vee-tay

to join
joindre
zhwan-druh

to jump
sauter
soh-tay

to keep
garder
gar-day

Sophie s'**amuse** !
Sophie is **having** fun!

to kick
donner un coup de pied
don-nay a(n)
koo duh pyay

to kill
tuer
tew-ay

to kiss
embrasser
ahm-bra-say

to know (someone)
connaître
kon-neh-truh

**to know
(something)**
savoir
sav-wahr

**to land
(in a plane)**
atterrir
at-tay-reer

to last
durer
dew-ray

to laugh
rire
reer

to leap
bondir
bon-deer

to learn
apprendre
ap-prahn-druh

to lie
mentir
mahn-teer

to lift
lever
luh-vay

to like
aimer
eh-may

to listen to
écouter
ay-koo-tay

to live
vivre
veev-ruh

a
b
c
d
e
f
g
Hh
Ii
Jj
Kk
Ll
m
n
o
p
q
r
s
t
u
v
w
x
y
z

Les grenouilles **sautent** haut.
Frogs **jump** high.

a
b
c
d
e
f
g
h
i
j
k

Ll
Mm
Nn
Oo
Pp

q
r
s
t
u
v
w
x
y
z

to lock
fermer à clé
fair-may ah klay

to look
regarder
ruh-gar-day

to look after
s'occuper de
sok-ew-pay duh

to look for
chercher
shair-shay

to lose
perdre
pair-druh

to love
adorer
ah-doh-ray

to magnify
grossir
groh-seer

to make
fabriquer
fah-bree-kay

to make a wish
faire un vœu
fair a(n) vuh

to make friends
se faire des amis
suh fair dez a-mee

to marry
se marier
suh mar-yay

to mean
signifier
see-nyee-fyay

to meet
rencontrer
rahn-kon-tray

to move
bouger
boo-zhay

to need
avoir besoin de
av-wahr buh-zwah(n) duh

to not feel well
ne pas se sentir bien
nuh pah suh sahn-teer bya(n)

to notice
remarquer
ruh-mar-kay

to offer
offrir
off-reer

to open
ouvrir
oo-vreer

to own
posséder
po-say-day

Lucie **ouvre** la porte.
Lucie **opens** the door.

to pack
faire les valises
fair lay va-leez

to paint
peindre
pan-druh

to pay
payer
pay-yay

to persuade
persuader
pair-swa-day

to pick up
ramasser
rah-mah-say

to plan
organiser
or-gah-nee-zay

to play
jouer
zhoo-ay

to play an instrument
jouer d'un instrument
zhoo-ay dan an-strew-mah(n)

to point
indiquer
an-dee-kay

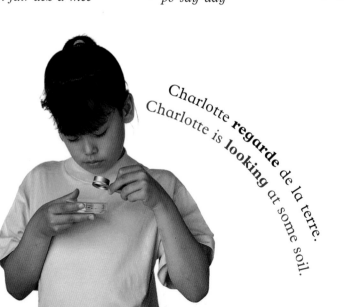

Charlotte **regarde** de la terre.
Charlotte is **looking** at some soil.

Peux-tu **peindre** un tableau ?
Can you **paint** a picture?

120

to pour
verser
vair-say

to practice
s'entraîner
sahn-treh-nay

to predict
prédire
pray-deer

to prefer
préférer
pray-fair-ay

to prepare
préparer
pray-pa-ray

to press
appuyer sur
ap-pwee-yay soor

to pretend
faire semblant
fair sahm-blah(n)

to print
imprimer
am-pree-may

to produce
produire
pro-dweer

to promise
promettre
pro-met-truh

to protect
protéger
pro-tay-zhay

to provide
fournir
foor-neer

to pull
tirer
tee-ray

to push
pousser
poo-say

to put
mettre
met-truh

to put away
ranger
rahn-zhay

to rain
pleuvoir
pluh-vwahr

to reach
atteindre
at-tan-druh

to read
lire
leer

to realize
se rendre compte
suh rahn-druh komt

to recognize
reconnaître
ruh-kon-neh-truh

to refuse
refuser
ruh-few-zay

to relax
se détendre
suh day-tahn-druh

to remain
rester
res-tay

to remember
se souvenir de
suh soo-vuh-neer duh

to repair
réparer
ray-pa-ray

to rest
se reposer
suh ruh-poh-zay

to return
revenir
ruh-vuh-neer

a
b
c
d
e
f
g
h
i
j
k
l
m
n
o
Pp
q
Rr
s
t
u
v
w
x
y
z

Verse l'eau doucement !
Pour the water in slowly!

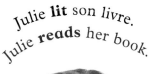

Julie **lit** son livre.
Julie **reads** her book.

121

a b c d e f g h i j k l m n o p q **Rr** **Ss** t u v w x y z

to ride a bike
faire du vélo
fair dew vay-lo

to ride a horse
monter à cheval
mon-tay ah shuh-val

to ring
sonner
so-nay

to roll
rouler
roo-lay

to rollerblade
faire du roller
fair dew ro-lair

to row
se promener en barque
suh pro-muh-nay ah(n) bark

to rub
frotter
fro-tay

to run
courir
koo-reer

to run after
poursuivre
poor-swee-vruh

to sail
faire de la voile
fair duh la vwal

to save
sauver
soh-vay

to say
dire
deer

**to score
(a goal)**
marquer
mar-kay

to scratch (oneself)
se gratter
suh grat-tay

to search
chercher
shair-shay

to see
voir
vwahr

to seem
sembler
sahm-blay

to sell
vendre
vahn-druh

I sell
je vends
zhuh vah(n)

you sell
tu vends
tew vah(n)

Mathieu **court** vite.
Mathieu **runs** fast.

he/she sells
il/elle vend
eel/el vah(n)

we sell
nous vendons
noo vah(n)-doh(n)

you (plural) sell
vous vendez
voo vah(n)-day

they sell
ils/elles vendent
eel/el vah(n)d

to send
envoyer
ahn-vwa-yay

to set the table
mettre la table
met-truh la tab-luh

to share
partager
par-ta-zhay

to shine
briller
bree-yay

to shout
crier
kree-yay

to show
montrer
mon-tray

Anna **semble** heureuse.
Anna **seems** happy.

Mélanie **monte à cheval**.
Mélanie **rides a horse**.

to sing
chanter
shahn-tay

to sit
s'asseoir
sass-wahr

to skate (on ice)
patiner (sur glace)
pa-tee-nay

to ski
skier
skee-yay

to sleep
dormir
dor-meer

to slide
glisser
glee-say

to slip
glisser
glee-say

to smell
sentir
sahn-teer

to smile
sourire
soo-reer

Clément **dort**.
Clément is **sleeping**.

to snow
neiger
nay-zhay

to sound (like)
sembler
sahm-blay

to speak
parler
par-lay

to spell
épeler
ay-puh-lay

to spin
tourner
toor-nay

to spread
étaler
ay-ta-lay

to stand
se tenir debout
suh tuh-neer duh-boo

to stand up
se lever
suh luh-vay

to start
commencer
kom-ahn-say

to stay
rester
res-tay

to stick
coller
kol-lay

to sting
piquer
pee-kay

to stop
arrêter
ah-reh-tay

to stretch
s'étirer
say-teer-ay

to study
étudier
ay-tewd-yay

to surf
surfer
suhr-fay

to surprise
surprendre
soor-prahn-druh

to survive
survivre
soor-veev-ruh

to swim
nager
na-zhay

a
b
c
d
e
f
g
h
i
j
k
l
m
n
o
p
q
r
Ss
t
u
v
w
x
y
z

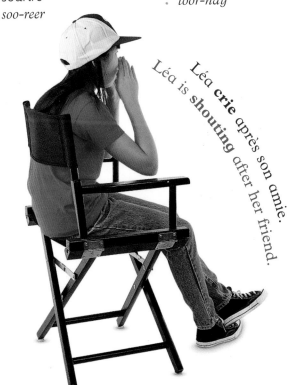

Léa **crie** après son amie.
Léa is **shouting** after her friend.

Étale le chocolat sur les gâteaux.
Spread the chocolate over the cakes.

123

a
b
c
d
e
f
g
h
i
j
k
l
m
n
o
p
q
r
s

Tt
Uu

v
w
x
y
z

*La fille **prend une photo**.
The girl is **taking a photo**.*

to take
prendre
prahn-druh

to take a photo
prendre une photo
prahn-druh ewn fo-toh

to take away
emporter
ahm-por-tay

to take turns
faire à tour de rôle
fair ah toor duh rohl

to talk
parler
par-lay

to taste
goûter
goo-tay

to teach
enseigner
ahn-sen-yay

to tease
taquiner
tah-kee-nay

to tell
raconter
rah-kon-tay

to tell a story
raconter une histoire
rak-on-tay ewn eest-wahr

to tell the time
dire l'heure
deer luhr

to thank
remercier
ruh-mair-syay

to think
réfléchir
ray-flay-sheer

to throw
jeter
zhuh-tay

to tidy up
ranger
rahn-zhay

to tie
attacher
at-ta-shay

to touch
toucher
too-shay

to train
s'entraîner
sahn-treh-nay

to translate
traduire
trad-weer

to travel
voyager
vwa-ya-zhay

to treat (well)
traiter (bien)
tray-tay bya(n)

to try (on)
essayer
es-say-yay

to turn
tourner
toor-nay

to type
taper
ta-pay

to understand
comprendre
kom-prahn-druh

to undress
se déshabiller
suh day-sa-bee-yay

to unpack
déballer
day-bal-lay

to use
utiliser
ew-tee-lee-zay

*Valérie **réfléchit**.
Valérie is **thinking**.*

*Jean **s'entraîne**.
Jean is **training**.*

to visit
visiter
vee-zee-tay

to wait
attendre
at-tahn-druh

to wake up
se réveiller
suh ray-vay-yay

to walk
marcher
mar-shay

to want
vouloir
vool-wahr

to warm
réchauffer
ray-shoh-fay

to wash
laver
la-vay

to wash (oneself)
se laver
suh la-vay

I wash
je me lave
zhuh muh lav

you wash
tu te laves
tew tuh lav

Manon fait **la vaisselle**.
Manon is doing **the dishes**.

he/she washes
il/elle se lave
eel/el suh lav

we wash
nous nous lavons
noo noo la-vo(n)

you (plural) wash
vous vous lavez
voo voo la-vay

they wash
ils/elles se lavent
eel/el suh lav

to wash the dishes
faire la vaisselle
fair la vay-sel

to watch
regarder
ruh-gar-day

to wave
faire un signe
de la main
*fair a(n) seen-ye
duh la ma(n)*

to wear
porter
por-tay

to weigh
peser
puh-zay

to whisper
chuchoter
shew-sho-tay

to win
gagner
gan-yay

to wish
souhaiter
sway-tay

to wonder
se demander
suh duh-mahn-day

to work
travailler
tra-va-yay

to work (function)
fonctionner
fonk-syo-nay

to wrap
emballer
ahm-bal-lay

to write
écrire
ay-kreer

a
b
c
d
e
f
g
h
i
j
k
l
m
n
o
p
q
r
s
t
u
Vv
Ww
x
y
z

Pierre **tape** sur son clavier.
Pierre is **typing** on his keyboard.

Julien **écrit** dans son journal.
Julien **writes** in his diary.

Expressions utiles
Useful phrases

Yes
Oui
wee

No
Non
no(n)

Hello
Bonjour
bon-zhoor

Goodbye
Au revoir
oh ruhv-wahr

See you later
À bientôt
ah byan-toh

Please
S'il te plaît (informal)
seel tuh pleh

S'il vous plaît (formal)
seel voo pleh

Thank you
Merci
mair-see

Excuse me
Excuse-moi
eks-kewz mwa

I'm sorry
Je suis désolé
zhuh swee day-zo-lay

My name is...
Je m'appelle...
zhuh ma-pel

I live in...
J'habite à...
zha-beet ah

I am... years old.
J'ai... ans.
zhay...ah(n)

I don't understand
Je ne comprends pas
*zhuh nuh
kom-prah(n) pah*

I don't know
Je ne sais pas
zhuh nuh say pah

Very well
Très bien
treh bya(n)

Learn the days of the week

Monday
lundi
lahn-dee

Tuesday
mardi
mar-dee

Wednesday
mercredi
mair-kruh-dee

Thursday
jeudi
zhuh-dee

Friday
vendredi
vahn-druh-dee

Saturday
samedi
sam-dee

Sunday
dimanche
dee-mahnsh

Very much
Beaucoup
boh-koo

I like/I don't like...
J'aime/Je n'aime pas...
zhehm/zhuh nehm pah

Let's go!
Allons-y !
alohn-zee

Happy Birthday!
Bon anniversaire !
bo(n) an-ee-vair-sair

Bonjour, je m'appelle Luc.

How are you?
Comment ça va ?
ko-mah(n) sa va

What is your name?
Comment t'appelles-tu ?
ko-mah(n) ta-pel tew

Do you speak...?
Parles-tu... ?
parl tew

Do you like...?
Aimes-tu... ?
ehm tew

Do you have...?
As-tu... ?
ah tew

Can I have...?
Puis-je avoir... ?
pwee zhuh av-wahr

How much...?
Combien... ?
kom-bya(n)

What's that?
Qu'est-ce que c'est ?
kess kuh say

How many?
Combien ?
kom-bya(n)

Can you help me?
Peux-tu m'aider ?
puh tew meh-day

What time is it?
Quelle heure est-il ?
kel uhr et eel

Help!
Au secours !
oh suh-koor

Stop!
Arrête !
ar-reht

Turn right/left
Tourne à droite/à gauche
toorn ah drwat/ah gohsh

Go straight ahead
Va tout droit
va too drwa

In front of
Devant
duh-vah(n)

Next to
À côté de
ah koh-tay duh

Where is/are...?
Où est/sont... ?
oo eh/so(n)

Allons-y !

Learn the months of the year

January
janvier
zhahnv-yay

February
février
fay-vree-yay

March
mars
mars

April
avril
av-reel

May
mai
may

June
juin
zhwa(n)

July
juillet
zhwee-yay

August
août
oot

September
septembre
sep-tahm-bruh

October
octobre
ok-to-bruh

November
novembre
no-vahm-bruh

December
décembre
day-sahm-bruh

Les nombres
Numbers

0	**zéro** *zay-roh* zero	10	**dix** *deess* ten	20	**vingt** *va(n)* twenty			

0 **zéro** *zay-roh* zero

1 **un** *a(n)* one

2 **deux** *duh* two

3 **trois** *trwa* three

4 **quatre** *kat-ruh* four

5 **cinq** *sank* five

6 **six** *seess* six

7 **sept** *set* seven

8 **huit** *weet* eight

9 **neuf** *nuhf* nine

10 **dix** *deess* ten

11 **onze** *onz* eleven

12 **douze** *dooz* twelve

13 **treize** *trez* thirteen

14 **quatorze** *kat-orz* fourteen

15 **quinze** *kanz* fifteen

16 **seize** *sez* sixteen

17 **dix-sept** *dees-set* seventeen

18 **dix-huit** *deez-weet* eighteen

19 **dix-neuf** *dees-nuhf* nineteen

20 **vingt** *va(n)* twenty

21 **vingt et un** *vant ay a(n)* twenty-one

30 **trente** *trahnt* thirty

40 **quarante** *kar-ahnt* forty

50 **cinquante** *sank-ahnt* fifty

60 **soixante** *swa-sahnt* sixty

70 **soixante-dix** *swa-sahnt-dees* seventy

80 **quatre-vingt** *kat-ruh-va(n)* eighty

90 **quatre-vingt-dix** *kat-ruh-va(n)-deess* ninety

100 **cent** *sah(n)* hundred

Acknowledgments

DK would like to thank Polly Goodman for proofreading.

The publisher would like to thank the following for their kind permission to reproduce their photographs:
(Key: a-above; b-below/bottom; c-center; f-far; l-left; r-right; t-top)

25 Dreamstime.com: Ilya Genkin (tc). 26-27 Dreamstime.com: Pressureua (c). Fotolia: Pablo Scapincahis / Arquiplay (ca). 29 Dreamstime.com: Buriy (tc); Marzanna Syncerz (cr). 31 www.aviationpictures.com/Austin J. Brown 1983 (tl); 31 Courtesy of FSTOP Pte. Ltd., Singapore (tc); 43 Dreamstime.com: Grafner (crb). 54 Corbis/Ronnie Kaufman (br) 55 Corbis/Craig Tuttle (tr); 55 Zefa/J. Jaemsen (cl); 55 Zefa/J. Jaemsen (cr); 55 Powerstock (bl); 72 Getty Images/ Stone/Stuart Westmorland (tl); 82 Indianapolis

Motor Speedway Foundation, Inc. (cb); 91 David Edge (tc); 91 Courtesy of Junior Department, Royal College of Music, London (br).
Cover images: *Front:* 123RF.com: Belchonock (clb); *Back:* **Dreamstime.com:** Skypixel (clb)

All other images © Dorling Kindersley. For further information see www.dkimages.com